SEARCHING
FOR
HIDDEN TREASURE

by Todd M. Price, M.D.

CONTENTS

NEPAL MAY 1990

Kathmandu • • Tempepla • Mount Everest

24 MAY

He was gaunt and wore faded pyjamas, yet color remained in his face that was surprisingly, full of joy. We were allowed no closer than five feet which was assured by the guard with his fixed bayonetted rifle. We could converse with Charles Mendes only through the doorway. Susan, his wife, and Neil Anderson, one of three brothers who in the future would facilitate much for us in Asia, had brought us to his cell. Other prisoners had visitors as well. The conversation was for all to hear. It was a conversation which revealed his freedom despite the constraing bars.

"Justin! So good of you to come! And Neily, good to see you again as well!" He shouted above the surrounding din. All seemed to stop speaking. A hush prevailed.

He continued, "Thank you so much for your support. Would you like something to drink?" A few of his fellow prisoners disappeared into the bowels of the prison to return forthwith holding bottles of lukewarm orange fanta which they offered for our enjoyment.

Justin attempted to decline but Asian hospitality prevailed upon us. This hospitality seemed out of place. We stood in front of a filthy, smelly prison. I supposed more rats than human occupants resided here and within the humans I wondered about the legions of parasitic worms and protozoa. As I contemplated these things, the warm soda fizzed for several minutes deep inside my intestinal tract.

"Charles, this is Dr. Price and Perry Adams. They are also from Lakewood. We hope to exert our influence to deliver you!" Justin instructed. After brief greetings between us, Justin continued. "We are praying for your quick release."

I quickly surveyed the prison and surrounding buildings. All were of brick construction. When we flew into Kathmandu, I noticed many brick factories with puffing smoke stacks encompassed by piles of similar clay bricks.

On top of the prison and other buildings, grass was growing from the mud roof. I wondered if such really protected against the monsoon rains. Thin slits in the brick served as the only ventilation during the summer, while in the winter these were open passageways for cold Himalayan gusts.

"I believe, because of your efforts and those of Christians around the world, I will soon be released. There seems to be a turn of events and a change in which the country is going," Charles said with exuberance. "The winds of freedom that have blown across Eastern Europe are beginning to blow here."

"What have the authorities said?" Justin asked.

"Previously they told me that if I requested a pardon, I would be out within minutes or at the most, days. But I refuse to ask for a pardon because to me that would be like admitting I was wrong. I am not in the wrong but in the right! I am not ashamed of preaching the Gospel of Jesus Christ!"

Later, we drove to Baktapur. The fields of Kathmandu valley were alive with ripe grain of various shades of green and yellow. They were alive also with workers who were manually bringing in the harvest.

Charles remained in his prison cell back in Kathmandu. Every day, Susan would bring him food and fresh clothing. Such "luxuries" were not provided him otherwise. His sentence was not for thievery or rioting. He was imprisoned because he attempted to manually bring in the harvest. He had simply told Nepalis about Jesus Christ. Because of such, he was sentenced to six years with no hope of parole.

25 MAY

"I've been up most of the night."

"What did you eat yesterday?" I asked. Before me in the Yak and Yeti coffee shop, sat a member of the delegation who was in Nepal to negotiate Charles' release. He had been describing his intestinal tract's woes.

"You didn't eat or drink from a roadside stand, did you?" I continued. Many of my patients who travel overseas and consult me for intestinal problems begin their demise by snacking at a roadside stand. I never understood the temptation. The food I had seen at these stands usually were covered with flies and\or were slowly fermenting in the hot sun. Yet people seem to think their stomach is made of iron.

"No. I know better than that," he responded. "But I did eat some fruit that Charles' jailmates offered when we were visiting yesterday."

I thought to myself, "He avoids roadside stands but thinks nothing of eating spoiled fruit from the jail?"

"Bad idea, huh?" he responded as if he could read my thoughts.

"Yep, bad idea. I don't think the jail's kitchen has recently passed the good housekeeping seal of approval. But we'll get something for you."

Soon I was in a local pharmacy and found some Bactrim. I was surprised to note that it was made by the very same company that marketed it in the states but it was at a fraction of the USA price. This got me to thinking about a project which we would institute on my next Nepal visit.

Later in the day we hired a taxi and a guide to take us to Nagarkot. We had been told that from that location just east of both Kathmandu and Baktapur, we actually would be able to see Mount Everest.

Between Kathmandu and Baktapur, workers had spread their harvest of grain on the road. As we and other vehicles passed over, the grain would be separated from the chaff. In Baktapur, we saw laborers cutting grain with a short handled scythe, necessitating constant bending and swinging. Others would throw what was cut into the air, another way to separate the grain from the chaff.

So it is in the Hindu Kingdom of Nepal. There are few workers. The work is hard, even backbreaking. But the fields are white, ready for harvest.

Beyond Baktapur, we began our ascent into the Himalayan foothills. Locals walked beside the road with large bundles on their backs, usually barefoot. Rain began to fall but both their work and their walking continued.

We came to a stop. The windshield wipers were failing. We took the opportunity to stretch our legs as the rain was but a sprinkle. Perry, an expert mechanic, attempted to help the driver with his wipers. But the driver repeatedly resisted his efforts. In short order, we resumed our journey yet at a slower pace. The wipers continued to malfunction.

As we gained altitude, the engine began to whine. It was a relief to us all when we came to the end of the road.

"You will need to walk the rest of the way," our guide said.

Up the mountain trail we ascended. Rocks of all sizes and shapes were in our path. Yet our goal was the top and we strode even faster, despite the obstacles.

Finally, we reached the top. Everest was in the clouds. So were we and I especially. Only a few years previously, I couldn't even walk out my front door without pain. I could hardly support my own weight. I crawled up stairs. But today, because of God's healing power, I walked up a mountain with ease. I was free of pain.

Enroute up to the road's end, our driver refused to accept the instruction and assistance of an expert mechanic who was in the car with him. Because of such, our journey was hindered.

Conversely, I did not refuse instruction and assistance when I was told of my degenerated hip. I humbled myself and prayed and sought God's face. My journey up the mountain path, therefore was not hindered, despite all the obstacles. I believe the same will be true for my journey of life, because God will be with me always.

I am glad God called me to be a physician. I am also happy that he gave me the ability and fortitude to become one. I am especially proud to be included within this group of dedicated men and women. I personally know many physicians who, if I were to call upon them to assist me with a sick patient, they would come and do all they could to help. They would do so whether it was day or in the middle of the night. They would get out of bed from a sound sleep without hesitation whether the patient had medical insurance or was an indigent. They would then stay as long as necessary.

I am also proud to report that a recent scientific survey among physicians reported that an incredible 95% of them believe in the power of prayer. We believe because we see God's hands move every day.

As a physician, I practice medicine. I was healed by God because I know, as do 95% of my colleagues, that God doesn't practice.

27 MAY

The room was cramped. Bags of grain occupied one wall. The other was occupied by an ever increasing number of Nepalis. They came in one or two at a time. Such was the precautions in a Hindu Kingdom in which changing one's religion demanded a prison term.

Not many weeks previously, hundreds of Nepalis grew tired of this anarchy. They longed for freedom and marched on the streets of Kathmandu. The policemen fired and the dead littered the streets. The outcry was great. Soon, the policemen turned from hunter to the hunted. They, too, died. By the time we had arrived, no policeman dared wear his uniform in public. Finally, the king granted concessions. Charles, however, had been arraigned under the old laws and was imprisoned.

Yesterday, we visited him once again. His spirits were undaunted. His joy was spreading across the prison as others began to catch Jesus. A revival of great proportions among the prisoners had broken out. Now, there was a new urgency among the authorities to pay more attention to the delegation of Christian Solidarity International who were daily presenting themselves to be heard. The authorities wanted Charles out of prison just as much as he longed to be: not necessarily because of the outcry of so called democratic nations about which which they cared little, but because the Jesus in Charles was breaking down the prison walls.

Yesterday also, I had seen pockets of Believers worship Jesus in spirit and in truth. I had given my testimony in a small Church of 200 faithful adherents. But I couldn't help but wonder whose testimony spoke the loudest, mine of healing, or theirs of standing strong for God in a most difficult place?

Today we were in an upper room far up in the Himalayas, hours from Kathmandu in a small town hugging the mountainside called Tempepla. Yet even here, the Hindu Monarchy still exacted severe penalties of religious intolerance. The prison was an ever present reality. Thus, the room filled slowly. Over an hour they came, one by one and two by two. Each came into the second story room the same way, single file up a creaking ladder.

Finally, the teacher began. He spoke in Nepali. He spoke in a whisper. All ears were upon him. No one stirred in anticipation, both in longing to hear of the God who required no more sacrifice, and in fear of being caught by the Hindu leaders of the village. Suddenly another creak came from the ladder. Immediately, all fell silent. The seconds crawled by. Only when one recognized as a Believer appeared through the attic door did everyone simultaneously sigh in relief.

The young, thin teacher resumed his discourse. Justin, Perry, and I understood none of his words. Occasionally, Neil wold interpret a phrase, but this was not enough to follow the sermon. As he progressed, He grew stronger and even bolder. His words became forceful and soon, no interpreter was necessary.

In Nepal, spirit bracelets are placed on a child at a very young age. They remain in place throughout life to supposedly protect against such things as disease and famine. No one dares remove them. The consequences, they believe, would be too great. In Nepal, there are prisons, like the one confining Charles. But there are even greater prisons which enslave a nation, signified by these bracelets.

The preacher had ceased his teaching. Now all Believers bowed, lifted hands, and worshipped the Almighty God. Soon, three made their way to the center of the room. Others surrounded to lay hands upon them. Their tears struck the dirty floor like thunderbolts. Their severed spirit bracelets smacked the ground with decisiveness and then were unceremoniously trodden under foot.

Tomorrow, Justin, Perry, and I would head for northern India. In a few weeks, Charles Mendies would walk free. But today, in the Himalayan Hindu Kingdom of Nepal on an insignificant mountain side village, we saw prison doors fall to earth.

NEPAL DECEMBER 1990
Pokhara ·
Kathmandu
· Kodari

1 DECEMBER

"Dr. Price, I hope you don't mind but would you please look at this woman? I've been keeping her and her family here in the church since last night when I found them on the street."

I turned to face the husband. From his unkempt, tattered clothes I recognized him as a poor mountain villager. He was nervously fingering an old leather string tied around his neck. I would soon learn that this was a 'spirit necklace' used to appease the 'gods'. His face was lined with fear and fatigue. Once he was told who I was, he immediately placed his hands together just beneath his chin and bowed slightly. When he looked up at me again, I could see the wrinkle in his brow, the tremor of his lip, and the tears in his bloodshot eyes. Before I even looked at his wife, I knew she was dying.

We had flown from Hong Kong, via Bangkok, only a few days previously. My wife, Sue, was six months' pregnant. Andrew, my young son at her side had yet to see his third birthday. His striking blond hair contrasted sharply with the black heads of the Nepalis; a trait that would continue to draw crowds wherever we went in Asia. Considering the high prevalence of tuberculosis, cholera, meningococcal meningitis and other contagious diseases in the Kathmandu valley, my medical colleagues back home in Texas assumed I had lost my senses for bringing both my son and my expectant wife. As I looked upon the woman, in the midst of another long agonal breath, I wondered what transmittable diseases she harbored and heard once again in my mind those many warnings from my fellow doctors.

Indeed, contagious diseases abounded in this Hindu kingdom. Only yesterday, Pam Seaward had taken us to the Infectious Disease Hospital. I had ventured inside with Pam, while my wife and son loitered outside with Pam's driver. We all thought it best not to expose either of them to the airborne pathogens that likely permeated the hospital corridors.

I had seen an open ward with patients on iron beds. Discolored sheets partially covered disease racked bodies but did little to absorb the microscopic droplets from coughing bronchi. There were many of these. I was comforted that Sue and Andrew had remained outside. On the far bed was a young girl with ecchymotic skin and glassy eye. Her head was deep inside the folds of a flat pillow. Intravenous tubing hung limply at her side, the end of which was inserted into an equally limp arm. It was quite obvious. She had meningococcal meningitis, a common ailment here in the crowded himalayan huts.

Just a few feet separated her from another woman who appeared equally moribund. She had similar sunken eye sockets and a thin arm with corresponding intravenous tubing. Her skin, however, was not ecchymotic but did have a salmon colored rash, especially on her exposed upper chest. Salmonella typhi had been cultured from her blood and stool and therefore she was also receiving intravenous ampicillin. Others in the room also had typhoid fever while one small boy had multiple lines into both arms. Cholera was his ailment. His doctors were racing to keep up with his fluid losses. They were optimistic for him, yet admitted that his younger sister and mother had not been so fortunate. His mother was already dead when she arrived in the arms of her husband. The sister was barely alive but so dehydrated that intravenous access had been denied despite multiple attempts. The father was at the bedside. His sorrow filled the room despite its enormity.

"They wait forever," Pam had said.

"Pardon me?" I had responded.

"They try spirit bracelets, strings tied around an arm or a leg. Then they try sacrificial offerings of eggs or even a chicken. If they are well off, they may even offer a goat, but most are not well off. Sometimes they pray to the mountain or the wind. If they are Buddhist, they spin prayer wheels and write prayers on flags. They believe, that as long as the wheel is turning or the flag is unfurled by the wind, that their prayers go up to heaven. Only when all else fails do they seek medical attention. They wait forever," she explained.

"Most don't reach the hospital alive," she added in the silence.

The medical resident herded us to the isolation ward which was located down several corridors. If they don't isolate meningococcal disease, tuberculosis, or typhoid fever, I had wondered to myself, what possibly do they isolate?

Finally, we approached a closed door. No masks were offered, nor gowns.

We entered a dark room with shades drawn and were simply asked to be as silent as possible. I recognized the disease immediately. A young boy was laying on his bed drooling. His eyes were open, filled with fear. The slightest stimulus, whether it be light, a sharp noise or a bump to his bed, precipitated vigorous muscle spasms with dramatic arching of his back and increased drooling. These were accompanied by pitiful moans of pain through the white foam at his lips. In the medical world, we called the back spasms, opisthotonos, and the disease, tetanus.

I had treated two tetanus patients back in the USA. We had sedated them and ensured their airway by intubation and placing them on a ventilator in a similarly darkened environment. We also guarded against pneumonia and treated the focus of infection, usually an unattended innocuous-appearing foot wound. A month later, the spasms would stop, allowing extubation and weaning from the ventilator.

But this boy would not survive. There was no ventilator nor endotracheal tube to prevent his eventual suffocation. His larynx would soon close due to spasms of surrounding muscles. Unfortunately, he would be fully aware, awake, and in constant pain until his end came. Pam and I had prayed silently and quickly departed. Our hope for him was a touch from Almighty God.

As we headed back outside we walked through damp and dark halls. Occasionally, each of us would almost lose footing on the slimy walkways.

Pam interrupted my thoughts by saying, "I can't believe this place!"

I, too, couldn't believe it. It was dirty, dank, and slimy everywhere. Patients who should have been isolated were in the same open ward. Infection control in this Infectious Disease Hospital was nonexistent.

But then Pam continued verbalizing her thoughts, "I can't believe it! They have really cleaned this place up!"

I decided against any further commentary.

Later in the day, Pam had taken us to a village not far from "Bouda", the Buddhist stupa with large foreboding eyes painted on the sides. On the way we had passed by multitudes of huts. We also passed by very modern appearing villas, with satellite dishes and other modern conveniences. Pam had indicated these were the homes of the high Buddhist lamas, or teachers.

In the village, clumps of cow dung dried on the outside walls of homes. They would be used as fuel for the evening fires. Nearby, butchered meat lay unprotected in the afternoon sun on wooden carts. The ubiquitous black flies frequented both the dung and the meat. Not far away, children congregated with their mothers around the local water well. I wondered about the boy with Cholera back at the hospital. A well such as this could have served as the focus of his infection. The flies probably playing a significant role in ensuring as many as possible receiving a good inoculum. Nevertheless, the children played, bathed, and drank. Open sewers along the street also served as their playground. No wonder, they all had pus flowing freely from their noses. It was a wonder to me that they were not all dead. God protects even the ignorant.

Thus my experience of the day before had already educated me. Disease in this valley was everywhere.

I turned to Pam, the resident missionary. The woman before me continued to gasp for every breath. "How long has she been like this?"

"Ever since I first found her on the street." She answered. "That's why I brought her here."

I had only met Pam at the airport when we arrived. Until then, I had no idea she even existed. Imagine my surprise when upon clearing customs I was met by this young westerner in the midst of a sea of Nepalis.

"Welcome to Nepal, Dr. Price," she had said, "we have heard so much about you."

I remembered mumbling a greeting. As she turned to direct her Nepali workers in rounding up the bags, I glanced back to my wife. My eyes questioned her as if to say, 'do we know her? '

But over tea in the coffee shop at the Yak and Yeti Hotel, we indeed began to know her as compassion for Nepal permeated her every word. I could picture in my mind this poor woman lying on the street, breathing her last, ignored by the crowds until Pam came by. Upon spotting her, Pam likely jumped from her seat commanding her driver to screech to a halt. As she gathered up the broken family from the dusty street, I could imagine traffic piling up behind Pam's old bus. The respective drivers would be cursing, fuming, and honking. The poor woman's well being was of no consequence to them.

The woman was propped up against one wall by several worn cloth bags. I assumed they to contained all her family's belongings. Her inspirations were quick and painful. Her expirations slow and easy. She was utilizing all her strength, grasping for every bit of oxygen possible. The strap muscles of her neck were straining, as likely were her chest-wall intercostals which were hidden by a dirty blouse. Her hair had thinned; her face gaunt and pale. She had glassy eyes, oblivious to the daylight. Grime from the Kathmandu street was plastered within each crevice of her face. I imagined her to be at least in her sixties. The small children clinging to her skirt were obviously her grand-children.

"How long has she been sick?" I asked.

While awaiting for Pam to translate my question to the family, I turned to find others gathering around as they arrived for the morning service. I assumed their looks of curiosity would soon turn to shock and disbelief upon seeing the woman's condition. Yet their faces revealed nothing of the kind. It was then that I realized that this must be a common occurrence in Pam's church. Those gathering simply began to pray and intercede.

"She's been like this since her last child was born."

"When was that?" I asked.

"About eight months ago." Now it was my turn to be in shock. The infant crawling near the sick woman's feet was not her grandchild, but her child!

"How old is she?"

"Thirty-five."

I turned to my wife who was now at my side. In my years of training and subsequent medical practice, I had seen many in this poor woman's condition; mostly in the intensive care setting. My wife as a critical care nurse had seen the same. We exchanged knowing glances. We knew her survival on this earth, barring a miracle, was extremely unlikely.

She wore the telltale 'spirit' necklaces, bracelets and anklets of a woman in bondage. These tattered pieces of leather with safety pins and beads signified subservience to demonic powers. I imagine that her entire life was one of trouble and misery because of this bondage. How many times had she shed tears over a child dying of pneumonia, or diarrhea, or measles? (Thirty per-cent of the children in these mountains died from such before they reached their fifth birthday.) How many times had she cancelled travel to get help for her current infection but delayed because these same gods would be offended? How many sacrifices of rice and chickens and maybe goats went to these gods which resulted in nothing but empty bellies on a starless night? How many divinations by the local shaman had to fail before she was desperate enough to travel the mountain roads to Kathmandu? Indeed, her gods had brought her to this place. She was about to step into eternal darkness. Death would not bring relief, only incomprehensible suffering without end.

"Has she seen a medical doctor?" I asked.

The husband produced a folded paper as Pam explained, "She has been to Bier Hospital but since she is a nonpaying patient, they discharged her."

I remembered Bier Hospital from a tour I had taken on a previous trip to Nepal. The dank hallways were filled with the smells of pus and human sewage. Through an open door I had viewed a patient with what appeared to be a dark, necrotic abdominal wound. Then, to my surprise, a nurse came close to the patient, waved over him, and the wound suddenly changed to a beefy red. The swarms of feeding flies had taken flight. I recalled my thoughts at the time as I headed for the closest exit with my mouth shut, 'in the event of sickness I would be air-evacuated to Singapore'.

I examined the paper and read her diagnosis, 'Probable tuberculosis'.

"They do this all the time!" Pam was saying with significant agitation. "I have pled and pled with the doctors in the past. But there are only a small number of beds reserved for indigent and they always seem to be filled."

I read further. "This says she was discharged with only 5 grams of hemoglobin!"

"Is that bad?" Pam asked.

"Normal is around 14." My wife answered. "We need to pray."

I took out my stethoscope to auscultate her lungs. "Filled with fluid and rhonchi." I reported. "Explain to her about Jesus and what He did for her. Also, explain to her that she is dying and nothing medically can be done to change the outcome."

When the husband comprehended the situation he fell to his knees at my feet, his eyes pleading for hope. His four children still were clutching their mother's tattered skirt. They were not making a sound. Their eyes were on their mother. Death was close.

Up until that moment, the woman had been staring into space. I assumed her to be oblivious to her environment; all her energy concentrating on each hard-fought breath. Yet her eyes suddenly fixed on mine, grabbed her husband and laboriously whispered between breaths in his ear.

"What did she say?" my wife asked.

The husband turned to Pam and explained. As he did, the others around us began to scurry about. One young man rushed upstairs and returned with a crude knife.

"They have been explaining to her before you arrived about Jesus." Pam was referring to the Nepali Christians that had been praying and ministering to her physical needs. "When she heard you say the same, she has decided to follow Jesus."

At that Pam went into a long discourse very slowly and deliberately in the woman's native Nepali. After several minutes, the woman held out her wrists with great difficulty. Immediately, the young man with the knife cut the bracelets. As he did, she dropped her arms like dead weights. He then did the same to the necklace and the anklets. The safety pins and beads fell and scattered aimlessly across the cement floor.

"I told her that she must totally turn from her gods. Therefore, she has consented and the bracelets were cut. This takes great courage and faith on her part. Most of these charms have been with her since childhood and she has never removed them.", Pam reported

She immediately began to breathe easier. Her husband watched for awhile. By this time many more had arrived, and the morning service was about to begin. My wife and I quickly prayed for her comfort. As we did, we both looked down to see our little blond-haired son placing his small hand on the woman's leg with his head bowed.

After giving instructions to keep her as comfortable as possible, we went into the next room where I was to speak. During the preliminaries, I occasionally checked in on her. On my third or fourth trip, I saw them cutting the leather strings on the husband's wrists. His head was bowed. He too, had entered the Kingdom.

Just before I was to speak, she suddenly worsened. Her breathing lost all rhythm, becoming very erratic. Pam realized the severity before I could verbalize.

"We must take her back to the hospital, immediately!" Pam was speaking. But her driver was not to be found. Several Nepalis scoured the neighborhood. A half hour passed and the woman's breathing pattern deteriorated. Suddenly the driver appeared at the door.

But he had no keys! Amid much gesticulation I could just imagine what was being said. Probably the round of blame of who had misplaced the keys. Nepalis scurried here and there. The keys remained elusive.

Finally, the driver started the bus with a nail.

"Shall I go with you?" I asked Pam.

"No. Stay here. It's almost time for you to speak. I'll take her and her husband. The children can stay with our workers."

Because of all the commotion, I was sure that my words would be empty. Yet many that day received Jesus. I'm glad that the Holy Ghost is not dependent upon my eloquence and ability. He's dependent only upon my availability.

Many hours later, Pam returned. My wife and I looked at her expectantly. It was obvious that she was fatigued by her slow, deliberate steps. We realized that the woman was dead. We were to discover later that her final diagnosis was extensive tuberculosis involving not only the lungs, but also the brain.

Her family will miss her. It is truly a tragedy that her time on earth, thirty-five years, was so short. Most of those years were spent in bondage to demon powers. Indeed her final hours were ones of severe torture at their hands. These powers that were behind her torment were anticipating an eternity of abuse. Yet her misery ended and her suffering ceased because she accepted Jesus. In the last minutes of life, she replaced the shackles of her 'spirit bracelets' with faith in the Living God. Today, she has the freedom to breathe the sweet aroma of uncontested victory.

2 DECEMBER

Kathmandu was a cow town. Not in the sense of the American west, although there was enough dust in the air to make one think that a cattle drive had just passed by. But Kathmandu's streets harbored cows that meandered unhindered searching for food. They usually found it in garbage that was piled almost everywhere. Nonchalantly they would pause to eat. Sometimes this would be in the middle of a busy street. It was of no concern to the cow. Traffic would divert.

We had diverted to avoid such a cow in the middle of one of Kathmandu's main streets. I don't know which street since none in town were marked. Our vehicle crept around "The animal" and then immediately veered to the right. With a lurch and a bump we parked.

The open door revealed a square with people, goats, and chickens everywhere. Garbage also was quite prevalent, thus the cows. My only surprise was the dumpster, which seemed quite out of place. My curiosity led me to peer inside. I wondered whether more garbage would be inside rather than out. I discovered the latter. I also discovered a man squatting in one corner reading the paper not far from a pile of goat entrails. I assume this dumpster was his refuge, which I chose not to disturb.

"It's on the other side of the square," Narayan indicated. Narayan led us through the crowd into a small alley on the opposite side of the square. As we entered the narrow passageway, we immediately moved to the side to allow a woman with a pile of brush and sticks piled high on her back to pass.

"Look, Mommie, a bush with legs!" Andrew yelled as the woman passed. Her load dwarfed her small frame and from behind, she indeed looked like a walking bush. Not too far down the alley, we met a man with a large office chair strapped to his back. We all marveled at how he could bear such a large load with a simple band strapped around his forehead. Then we noticed his wife who was walking twenty feet to his rear. She too had a band wrapped around her forehead. However, on her back was not a mere office chair. Her frail frame supported the weight of a large office desk.

"Women sometimes are treated like animals and bear unbelievable burdens," Narayan explained. He had noticed our astonished faces. I had also noticed similar regard for women since arriving. At the airport, I noticed a man with an umbrella. His wife, however, walked fifteen feet behind him without an umbrella in the drizzling rain.

"We are here," Narayan announced.

We entered the small office of a pharmaceutical distribution company. Justin handled the transaction, securing enough antibiotics, analgesics, vitamins, antiparasitics, and ointments to treat 1200 people at a fraction of the USA cost.

Back at the Yak and Yeti, we sorted the medications, packaging them into twenty kits. These would serve as the basis for the evening's instruction.

Night fell. Pam's bus arrived. Through the dark streets we rode, bumping and swaying. Finally we came to a squeaking halt. Outside, the dust was heavy. Darkened huts lined the road. On the mountainsides surrounding us, campfires of a thousand family shacks twinkled in the night. Smell of woodsmoke penetrated the darkness.

We all stooped low and entered the Church. Our shoes came off, as is the custom. Twenty evangelists and pastors sat on the Tibetan rugs. They had been chosen by their respective leaders to receive medical instruction and the medications we had gathered into kits.

The Nepalis whose campfires we had seen on the mountainsides were sick. They had no access to medical care because no doctor nor nurse would go there. The only ones who would go to these villages were the ones sitting before me. But they had gone before and had been stoned. This Hindu Kingdom wanted nothing to do with their message of a loving God. Centuries of tradition and beliefs dictated their actions. These traditions and beliefs had also dictated their sicknesses.

We believed that by equipping these Christian workers with medical knowledge and medications, the mountain people would welcome them. Then, they could hear and see the Gospel message demonstrated.

We taught.

The spiritual wickedness that had ruled in these high places would soon find their jurisdiction threatened.

3 DECEMBER

"Narayan has arranged with the local health authorities for you to examine patients. Pam's bus will be here shortly to pick us up."

Justin had indicated the day's plans as we stood in the lobby of the Yak and Yeti. I had hoped to see a group of patients to better judge the medical needs of a typical Nepali village. Justin, as usual, had done well. As the administrator of Lakewood Church, he had also ensured that we obtain the best possible exchange rate for Lakewood's donated money to purchase the medications.

With the usual fanfare of squeaking shocks and billowing exhaust pipe, Pam's bus arrived. When Pam jumped to the sidewalk, Andrew immediately greeted her.

"Hi, Ham!" Andrew was still having difficulty pronouncing his "P's". Good naturedly, Pam exchanged greetings with us all.

Narayan was with her and sat directly behind the driver to provide directions. Narayan had been born to a high cast Brahmin family in southern Nepal. Now he was responsible for several local pastors, ensuring that their financial support was administered correctly. On our last visit to Nepal, he had proudly shown Justin and I his spartan living quarters which he shared with a local evangelist. To warm water for a cup of tea he had used a bunsen burner, which is what he also used to cook. At that time we discovered that he had declined offers to go to the USA. Instead, he sought to serve God here in this primitive setting.

We passed by the University. It was here that Pam studied Nepali and Tibetan,

16

thereby ensuring her student visa status. Otherwise, she would face prompt deportation despite her years of providing homes for the orphans here in Kathmandu. Seventeen years previously, she had arrived from Singapore where she had grown up with missionary parents. She came to assist a single woman missionary. The older missionary had since left the country but Pam had stayed. Many had been her adventures for Christ among mountain villages of Nepal and Tibet. The local government had been far from supportive and had taken every opportunity to hinder her, even demanding jail time from her on several occasions. Nevertheless, she persevered for God's call on her life. Because of her, many had not died and thousands had heard for the first time about Jesus Christ.

Once we passed the Outer Ring Road, we began our jostling over dirt pathways. Soon we came to a halt. Narayan arose to announce our arrival.

The village was of brick and mud construction. Most structures were three stories. The bottom mud floor was where the animals stabled. A rickety ladder led to a wood floor littered with hay, stubble, and bags of harvested grain. The top floor served as sleeping quarters. No floor was very well illuminated as only small slits in the wall allowed rays of sunshine. The roof was flat, allowing for additional living space on warm evenings, which at this elevation was extremely rare. Grass and weeds also grew from the mud roof in many locations.

From the roof one could look out across the fields of cut barley and other grains. They were of different shades of brown although back in May they were a verdant green. The field's backdrop were the ever present himalayas. The slopes were gentle from afar yet murderously steep and uninviting up close. A haze blanketed the sky obscuring the jagged snow covered peaks of the higher elevations.

Back on the ground were the open sewers which ran amongst and between the homes. Children played barefoot. Goats defecated nearby. In the middle of the pathway, a foul smelling trickle of water undoubtedly carried the teaming bacteria that I was asked to eradicate from those who sought my exams.

The local health post was a small one room building, as dark inside as the mud and brick used to construct it. The cabinets were empty. Only my instruments and the medications we had earlier bought in nearby Baktapur would allieviate any suffering.

I would examine sixty. Sixty would have intestinal parasites. Sixty were malnourished. Sixty complained of diffuse body aches. None went away empty handed. We provided medication for all.

Evening came. We had departed the Newari village and arrived back at Pam's Church. My shoes were off allowing my white socks the freedom to become black. I was at the podium facing a room packed with Nepalis, women on one side and men on the other. Everyone had a cough. I briefly wondered what Andrew and Sue would contract.

Outside, the horns of local Buddhist monasteries called the faithful to worship. Inside these, would be smoke, chanting and frenzied divination.

But within the Church I spoke of a God who required not sacrifice but obedience.

"I have seen many here in Kathmandu over the past few days who are crippled, not because they were born that way nor were injured, but because they had dedicated their good legs to their gods. In return, they became lame from atrophied and contracted legs, forced to beg for survival."

I paused to let this truth, known to everyone in the building, sink in. Then I continued.

"But I, on the other hand, dedicated my degenerated leg to Jesus Christ. In return, He restored me and gave me back a well functioning leg. I am not crippled and I do not beg."

"The heathen gods take good legs and make them bad. Jesus Christ took my bad leg and made it good. Who do you want to serve?"

When I paused, the horns blared no more. The chants were silent.

Within Pam's Church, no one went away empty handed.

4 DECEMBER

Guine had accompanied us. He was one of three brothers, all serving God together. Their ministry began here in Nepal but has since spread across Asia. They, too, chose to labor among Asia's millions rather than seek the life of ease. Andrew loved him and chose to go with him up the side of the mountain.

"Look at your mother! See? Way down by the road sitting on a rock." Guine was pointing to Sue sitting just behind the broken down bus.

"Mommie! Mommie! Up here!" Andrew yelled. We all began to wave with our arms outstretched. To my surprise she heard and began waving back.

We were on a 45 degree incline surrounded by small brush and grass. The bus had already suffered several mishaps: temporary loss of brakes, a fractured tie-rod, and now a flat tire. While the Nepalis replaced the tire, Guine, Andrew, and I began to stretch our legs. Sue decided to do the same but with much more wisdom. She was relaxing on a smooth boulder next to the road, behind the disabled bus and just above a rushing mountain stream while we struggled up the side of the mountain. Realization of our precarious situation only occurred when the bus' horn blew announcing its road-worthiness once again. We soon began slipping and falling down the steep grade.

Hereafter, our journey would be much slower until we arrived at the village on the Tibetan border. There, the bus would require welding and a brake check.

We had left Kathmandu at 7:00AM. Several hours of hard riding had brought us to Dhulikhel where we took breakfast. The fog had not cleared until we finished our stale toast and jam. Only then could we appreciate the stark elevations.

The rugged road which hugged the mountain side had thus far been far from friendly. Potholes abounded. In many places the summer thaw had led to avalanches wiping out the road. In these locations, hastily built detours violently rocked the bus. With each turn, and there were many, rugged peaks rose to even greater heights. Fortunately for us, the winter snows had not yet fallen.

Back on the bus, Pam related some of her experiences and associated tribulations living for Christ here in the Himalayas. Justin, too, had similar stories regarding his travels to the eastern block nations.

Finally, we arrived in Kodari in time for a late lunch served in a crude, dark roadside cafe. Goat entrails were drying on the wall. We chose instead to have a package of noodles boiled for us in a huge crock pot located on the floor. We all filtered outside when our bowls emptied.

Strings of flags which were draped over the roadway every ten to fifteen feet indicated that the entire town had just completed a celebration to some heathen god. On the sidewalk, stone idols were stained red with chicken and goat blood. An oppressive spirit prevailed.

Justin bent down and whispered in Andrew's ear. Suddenly, Andrew jumped up and began skipping down the side of the street, singing, "Jesus Loves Me". His blond hair soon drew a crowd of dark haired boys and girls. Their parents followed. Pam, Guine, and Narayan took the opportunity to explain the Gospel.

Later in the day, I again gave my testimony in a darkened upper room to a crowd of Nepalis. Among these was a young girl whose brief life had been full of torment. The heathen gods which the townspeople served gave her no peace, only abuse. Out of her tribulations she had called out to God. She had heard from someone about Jesus. Not knowing too much about Him, she had for many nights stayed up late praying that He may send someone to tell her more.

I told her more.

Down on the street, the cool Himalayan wind whipped the flags into a frenzy and the cold, stone idols remained covered with goat and chicken blood.

In this upper room, however, there was no frenzy, only peace. Several, including the young girl, had believed. They were now covered, not with the blood of animals, but by the blood of the Lamb.

5 DECEMBER

By late morning we were at Pashupati. It was here on the banks of the Bagmati River, a tributary of the Ganges, that local Hindus brought their dead, and near dead, for burial preparations. Buildings with one side open to the west riverbank served as holding areas, where relatives brought the near dead. Once the last breath had been taken, mourners would wail, male relatives would have their heads shaved, and the body draped with cloth. A pyre of sandalwood would then be carefully constructed on cement platforms which dotted the river edge. The body was lifted atop this pyre and set ablaze and the resulting ashes ceremoniously pushed into the holy river below. Monkeys darted about from pyre to pyre and temple to temple, which also littered the river's banks. They would defecate and urinate into the holy river. Downstream, holy men and other worshippers bathed in and drank from this same riverwater.

Shrill wailing came from across the river. Guine's good natured smile had faded and tears filled his eyes. "Another one has entered eternity unprepared," he solemnly announced. Behind us a holy man dressed in a loincloth, his hair wrapped with cow dung, was sitting on a temple's steps instructing a small group of westerners. Pam, Justin, and Narayan were across the bridge closer to the source of the wails. They, too, were silent observers of this most dreadful scene. A choking oppressive atmosphere mixed with the smell of burning flesh filled our nostrils.

"We better go," Justin approached.

We silently filtered to the bus and headed for the domestic airport.

For some reason, the driver took us back into central Kathmandu. We were soon on Kanti Path, one of the main streets of downtown. We passed by the infamous Bier Hospital and soon thereafter came the military garrison of the Royal Gurkha Rifles. Not too many meters later we passed by the jail, where Justin and I had spent so much time on our last visit.

We finally arrived at the domestic terminal of Tribhuwan Airport. To our surprise, Charles Mendes was there to meet us. We had visited with him earlier in the week at his orphanage. He looked much healthier than he did on our last visit to Nepal when he was holed up in the jail we had just passed by.

"You'll have a great time in Pokhara," Charles said. "It is truly the garden spot of Nepal. The mountains are very beautiful and many westerners begin their treks from there."

"That's exactly what Pam said," Justin added. "But we are going there mostly to encourage the believers."

Flight time had come and gone, yet our plane hadn't. Previous experience with schedules in Nepal had taught us that time here is relative. We relaxed at our table at the coffee shop, catching up with news about works in western Nepal, close to Pokhara.

Ultimately, an announcement in Nepali via the static-filled public address system prompted Charles and Pam to hurry us toward our gate, which happened to be the only gate.

Andrew caught a ride on Justin's back. Narayan, Sue, and I followed across the tarmac to our waiting Royal Nepali Airways plane. One by one, we climbed the ladder towards the rear of the plane which led into the passenger cabin. Inside, the seats were of the fold-down bench type, each holding two passengers. After everyone was seated, the lone stewardess came to the front of the cabin with a tray of hard candy and a wad of cotton. I took some candy but no cotton, as I had little idea of its purpose. When the engines started, I quickly realized the utility of such and yelled back to Narayan over the noise to grab an extra wad for Sue and I.

We were airborne quickly and surprisingly enjoyed a smooth ride. Enroute, we flew through mountain passes and appreciated the enormity of this mountain range with much better clarity. Looking down at the rugged terrain, I understood why the average life-span here had not yet climbed above the mid-forties. Below us, smoke from remote villages rose to greet us.

We landed with a few preliminary bounces on a grass strip and came to our final resting place in front of a shed that served as Pokhara's airport terminal.

We were instructed to standby while the lone baggage handler wrestled our bags one by one from the cargo bin and threw each at our feet on the grass. Thereafter, as far as he or anyone else was concerned, we were on our own.

We lugged our bags across the grass, then onto the street, and finally to the hotel. Along the road were red and white poinsettia bushes rising ten to twelve feet. Beyond them loomed the ice and snow covered Annapurna Himal Range, nicknamed "fishtail" because of appearances. The peaks rose higher than I could have imagined possible, which made me feel very insignificant.

Once inside the hotel we were showed to our rooms. Our ascent up one flight of stairs led to a long hallway with a single fixture-less light bulb as the only source of illumination. Despite the resulting shadows, we could see into the kitchen as we passed by the open side door. A worker was squatting, as Asians commonly do, drying some dishes with a rag. Suddenly, he placed the rag on the floor, wiped his nose with his hand, retrieved the rag and continued his drying job.

Sue looked at me and with no expression simply stated, "That's it, I'm not eating here."

I presented no argument.

Our rooms were furnished with two iron beds and a nightstand in between. The only wall decoration was a painting of shiva, a hindu god. I promptly removed shiva and placed her inside a closet facing the wall.

A knock at the door revealed Justin, whose room was next door.

"Let's try something," Justin ventured. "Yep, just as I thought. My skeleton key also fits your door."

"That makes me feel real secure," I sarcastically added.

"What do you say we go find a better hotel?" Justin asked.

"I'm all for that," Sue agreed.

Downstairs, Justin attempted to get the receptionist to call for a cab. Sue, Andrew, and I headed for the front door. Justin soon joined us to report that the receptionist advised we walk. Suddenly, a cab appeared and deposited a Japanese tourist on the doorstep. Justin quickly maneuvered in front of the cab, while we piled into the back seat. Justin claimed the front seat beside the driver. As we pulled away, Justin said, "Take us to the best hotel in town!"

The driver turned with a look of astonishment, "But, sir, you are at the best hotel in town." He placed great emphasis on "at".

An uncomfortable pause ensued during which time I examined the driver's face. I could imagine that his thoughts were saying, "..and how much more luxury can you westerners want?". Then I added, "Well, just show us a few other hotels nearby."

By this time darkness had fallen. In the Himalayas, when darkness falls, it crashes. There was no moon, but plenty of bright stars. Nevertheless, the night was black. The dim lights of the taxi illuminated little. Darkness here was overpowering.

The first hotel was in the middle of a lake. The only way of getting there was on a leaking raft, piloted by a frail old man with an equally frail pole. We decided against venturing out onto the lake under those conditions. We viewed a room at the next hotel. But it was already occupied by scorpions which scurried across the bedsheets when the light came on.

"Okay, you're right," I conceded to the cabby. "But how about taking us to a local restaurant?" I was thinking about Sue's earlier pronouncement regarding the restaurant back at our hotel.

"I can take but I cannot wait. And you will probably have to walk back to the hotel."

"Why's that?" Justin asked.

"Because taxis stop running at 8:00PM."

"Why's that?" Sue asked.

"It's too dangerous."

"Why is it too dangerous?" It was my turn to do the asking.

"Well, at the end of the day people start smoking weeds, their thinking becomes cloudy and they start attacking everything that moves. I know some friends who have had their taxis rolled by gangs of such hooligans."

We soon found ourselves back at our hotel. Fortunately, we had some granola bars in our bags up in our room.

Upon entering, I found shiva back on the wall. I again removed her and placed her in her rightful spot for the evening, face towards the wall in the closet.

6 DECEMBER

"Garden City or not, we need to get out of here!"

"I'm all for that," Sue responded to Justin's suggestion.

"What do you think, Todd? I'm sure Narayan will understand. Something tells me that we better get back to Kathmandu as quickly as possible!"

I sat silently in the back seat. Justin's suggestions were well put. Ever since arriving here I had felt an uneasiness.

"Okay. If we can rearrange our tickets for today, we'll leave," I responded.

Justin immediately walked across to the airport. Sue and I remained at the hotel with Andrew where we hurriedly gathered our things and checked out.

Justin was not long. "They said that we might be able to fly standby on the 3:30PM flight back to Kathmandu. The earlier we get there, the more likely we'll be on that flight."

"No problem. We can go now. We've already checked out," I answered.

At the one room "terminal", we signed in. No one assured us of a seat, yet at 2:30PM, they weighed our bags and issued boarding passes. Shortly thereafter, a plane landed and we walked out on the grass with the other passengers. At 3:00PM we were airborne.

We were amazed. Not only had we made the flight, it had left early. After much discussion among ourselves trying to figure it out, Justin finally asked a fellow passenger sitting behind him.

When Justin turned back around, he was laughing.

"What's wrong?" I asked.

"Nothing," Justin answered. "It's just that this is not the 3:30PM flight. It's the 9:30AM flight."

8 DECEMBER

I jumped onto Pam's bus for the last time. Justin, Andrew, and Sue were already aboard. Our bags were in the back seat. Before I sat down, Sue motioned towards a Nepali woman and her son whom I did not recognize sitting immediately behind the driver. The son had a filthy orange bandanna across his left eye. His right eye had an opacified cornea. He obviously was blind. The mother held him close. They were both dressed in rags.

"I just picked them up from Thamel," Pam advised. Thamel was the area of town where many beggars congregated. Other congregated there as well. A section of Thamel had been nicknamed "Freak street" back in the sixties because so many expatriots from the west congregated there to smoke weed and exchange drugs in their tie-died clothing and long unkempt hair. Even today, Thamel was where drugs could be bought and rooms let for less than the price of a Big Mac in Hong Kong. Occasionally, you could see someone who had not yet escaped the sixties wandering down the narrow street.

Others who wandered here were the beggars, including this mother and son.

"Could you look at the boy's eye?" Pam asked.

Gently, Pam assisted the mother as she removed the bandanna. Underneath, the eye was proptotic, bulging out of the socket. It was hopelessly infected and necrotic.

"We need to get him to the hospital as soon as possible!"

"But that's where he just came from," Pam answered. "He was discharged earlier today. The father has abandoned them and with nowhere to go, the mother was begging on the street. The Holy Ghost prompted me to stop."

"Well, they need to get back into the hospital or else the boy may die."

"You don't understand, Dr. Price. They can't go back."

"Why not?"

"Because he was discharged."

"How can they discharge him in such a condition?"

"They just do. Remember, you are not in America." Then Pam continued. "He was admitted for correction of a cataract of his right eye. But they operated on the wrong eye and infection set in. Now he can see out of neither."

After a long pause, I responded. "He needs cephalexin at this dosage." I handed Pam a piece of paper with the written dosage and some rupees to cover the cost. "But what he needs really is a miracle."

Sue grabbed Andrew's hand, and as they did for the dying woman in Pam's church a few day previously, they laid hands on the boy and began to pray.

Several hours later, we were safely aboard the Thai jet heading over the mountains for Bangkok. Had we not come back from Pokhara when we did, we would not have made this flight. Soon after we had arrived back in Kathmandu, the pilots of Royal Nepali Airways went on strike. In effect, we were on the last flight. In addition, there had been a problem with our tickets on Thai Airways. Had we not come back that day, we would have been stranded. Guine was not so fortunate. His departure from Kathmandu was delayed two weeks. It must have been the Holy Ghost that placed that uneasiness within us. Because we followed His urging, we were back on schedule, breathing easier and headed for Bangkok.

On the other side of Sue, Andrew was enjoying the packet of games and toys the stewardess provided. Justin was reading a few rows to our rear.

"Do you think we did the right thing by bringing Andrew?" Sue asked.

I secretly had wondered the same, but I found myself answering, "Andrew will be fine."

"How about the baby?"

My answer came not so quickly. I thought about all the places we had been and the high prevalence of airborne infectious diseases such as meningitis and tuberculosis. I also recalled how Sue had been in the midst of most every situation, (including enclosed churches with everyone coughing and sneezing) praying and interceding. She also spent a lot of time with the women and children, who preferenterally approached her rather than myself. I suppose they could sense both her compassion and empathy: she could relate to their needs. They would also ask via interpreters about the baby, which resulted in a lot of smiles and nods of understanding without words on both sides of the conversation.

But I simply reaffirmed her faith in God's promises to protect her by saying, "The baby will be fine." Three months later God would reward her faith by providing a healthy baby boy, named Austin.

"I can't get over that little boy with the eye infection. Do you think he will make it?" Sue asked. Her compassion for the downtrodden again was surfacing.

"Nope. Not unless God intervenes."

After a short pause, I added, "But knowing Pam, she will see to it that He does."

NEPAL MARCH 1992

Kathmandu

11 MARCH

The Thai Airways airbus had begun its precarious descent. Although this would be my third trip into the Hindu Kingdom, I remained leery of the final approach into Kathmandu's international airport. Actually, the airport was little more than a single airstrip in the middle of Kathmandu valley surrounded by lofty himalayan peaks. A few months later this very flight, and possibly this very airbus, would fall much short. Days would be required to recover all the bodies spread across rugged terrain. Today, I did not know of this future tragedy. I simply knew the approach as usual would be a bit bumpy. Outside, the peaks seemed to lunge out for the fuselage that fortunately, was just out of reach. The pilots were doing their very best to follow the single radio beam to the safety of the runway.

Between bumps, I completed my embarkation card. As I did, I noticed the red print, '...medications valued over 150 rupees must be declared...'. This roughly equated to $5. Further down the card I read that failure to declare could result in fines, confiscation of goods, and even imprisonment. I recalled the Nepali prisons that I had visited in the past. On those occasions, I was glad to be a visitor.

Inside my suitcase, I had antibiotics worth over $10,000. To declare would guarantee confiscation. Not to declare could lead to the problems as stated above. I prayed. God would simply have to intervene. I was planning not to make a profit but rather to freely give them to the sick. A healthy customs agent, who likely would sell them at a big profit, was not my intended recipient.

Touchdown interrupted my thoughts and stimulated me to more prayer. As we transferred to a waiting bus on the tarmac, a gust of the cool Himalayan

March wind struck my face. Once we were all crammed inside, the bus jerked away from its position. Only a few had seats. Most of the rest of us grabbed onto the overhead bars for equilibrium in the shifting vehicle. We were eventually deposited just outside the familiar entryhall, where we scrambled to fill out the required visa applications. Everyone who had been here before knew the sluggish bureaucratic agents would unenthusiastically attend to their duties and thereby create a long, snail-paced queue. Those first-time visitors meandered around aimlessly since there were few visible instructions to the expected entry procedure.

Even though I knew what was expected, many had completed the paperwork ahead of me resulting in my position towards the line's end. Finally, after a long wait, I produced my papers, passport, and fifteen American dollars. The agent stamped my passport in his slow and deliberate pace. Soon I was on my way to claim my bag: the bag with the medicines hidden inside.

My fellow passengers loitered around the claim area. There were no moving belts or automated baggage delivery here, simply two holes in the wall covered by strips of fabric. Porters shoved the off-loaded baggage through these. I soon found my bulging bag off to the side. I immediately pulled it towards the only available customs agent and then hoisted it to his vacant table.

"Nothing to declare?" he asked as I handed him my papers.

Previously in my mind I had rehearsed my answer to such a question. But now that it was spoken, my vocal cords wouldn't work. My throat was as dry as sandpaper in a sandstorm. He felt around the bulging bag. I thought about the horror stories from others, who under similar circumstances had been detained and interrogated for hours and even days. I was hoping that my years of training in medical school and postgraduate studies would pay off. It was there where I learned to cloak my thoughts with a nonchalant visual appearance. After all, it was only when my professors saw the fear and sweat in my eyes would they come in for the kill.

The agent's trained hands felt for contraband. As I watched him work it was as if the small lumps in the bag were as big as the himalayas that surrounded us. Suddenly, it seemed he had detected a suspicious bulge. He bent closer for a more careful feel, his brow furrowed with concentration. As he turned to face me, I simply knew he was going to confront me. My imagination anticipated the chain of events. He would open my bag, spilling out my precious medications. Such would attract the attention of other agents as well as the uniformed Gurkha at the doorway, who would draw a weapon and train it on me. The other passengers would stop and stare. Those behind me would scatter.

Thereafter, my real agony would begin.

He turned to me and smiled. "Welcome to Nepal," he said as he directed me towards the exit.

I briefly paused. But then I hoisted my bags and departed quickly.

12 MARCH

He was only 29 and he had anasarca. My grandmother would have called it 'the dropsy'. Simply put, he was grossly edematous everywhere. His swollen face reflected his misery and discomfort. Just a few steps would leave him severely short of breath; the extra weight of the fluid in his legs taxed his already overburdened cardiovascular system.

They had come from every district in Nepal, parts of India and even Bhutan. The previous evening, those from the Indian state of Nagaland had adorned themselves in their colorful native dress and had entertained everyone with their songs. I remembered not understanding any words but comprehending their message. It was not difficult to appreciate from their zeal how Nagaland had evolved from a tribal area of headhunters to one where Christ was transforming thousands.

The Bhutanese delegation had traveled first by foot for several days, then by bus. The bus ride ended abruptly a few days after it began when the vehicle veered too close to another. Two of their number were severely injured in the collision and transported to a local medical station (as the nearest hospital was days away over narrow mountain roads). The remainder decided to proceed and arrived in Kathmandu seven days after they had originally departed. To them, Kathmandu was like Manhattan which they viewed with eyes of wonder. I considered it little more than a dusty frontier town with unmarked streets and open sewers.

The morning session was over. Those who were sick had sought me out. One exam seemed to beget another and soon an impromptu clinic had evolved. Most had coughs, sinus infections, and the usual aches and pains. The medications I had brought had indeed come in handy, as did my stethoscope and otoscope.

The last young man in line was the one described above. He knew he was seriously ill and needed help. After my exam, I agreed. He appeared to be suffering from nephrotic syndrome and needed acute hospitalization. In the best of circumstances, a battery of blood tests, as well as possibly a kidney biopsy would be necessary to arrive at a diagnosis. Yet once diagnosed, his cure may prove to be elusive. Although this room in the back of the church was not the best of circumstances, Bier Hospital in downtown Kathmandu would not be much better. He needed much more than what the Nepali medical system could offer.

"I believe you are seriously ill," I began. "I think you have something affecting your kidneys. But I am sorry to say that I have no medicine that will help you."

His big brown eyes returned a glassy stare. I could only guess his hidden thoughts. On the surface I could see his physical problems, classically described in the medical literature. But he was not just a textbook case; he was not a machine. He was a human being; a person whose illness had effected everyone close to him. After all, none of us live to ourselves, nor die to ourselves. His life, like mine, effects many others. I wondered how his illness had effected his parents. Yet likely in this country of abbreviated lifespans, his parents were already dead.

His wife was probably influenced the most by his illness. All she could do, however, was watch him suffer and worry about its consequences. What changes had come upon his children as they feared the unknown that his suffering had fostered? Likely, they would all, too soon, if not already, be forced to beg on the streets for sustenance. Unfortunately, they would not be alone. The social programs in Nepal are few.

He nodded his head slowly. Most assuredly, he had suspected something was terribly wrong. His head bowed in disappointment. He probably had hoped for an injection or pill that would return him to health.

"But all hope is not lost!" I responded. "Remember, we have a God who cares for you. His Son, Jesus, is still alive and will help you. Do you believe this?"

His watery eyes looked straight into mine as he confirmed his belief.

"Then let's pray!" With that, I began. I laid my hands on his shoulders. Soon others came to join our prayer as they passed by. Each prayed in his or her own language as I prayed aloud in English.

I finished. When his eyes once again met mine, they were moistened, streaking his grimy face. Before he left, he grabbed my shoulders, at first hesitantly, but then with surprising strength. He regained his composure, stepped back and placed his hands together in the more typical 'namaste' expression of gratitude.

He slowly shuffled to the door.

13 MARCH

The Rana family ruled Nepal for over one hundred years, not as kings and queens, but as prime ministers. In 1847, the first Rana was appointed Prime Minister by the then King Shah. Unbeknownst to the King, Prime Minister Rana would consolidate his power and soon hold the royal family under house arrest. Thereafter, the royals would be puppets whose strings were pulled tightly by the Prime Minister. Rana's son would rule after him, with subsequent sons and grandsons inheriting the prime minister post thereafter. Until 1951, when King Tribhuvan Shah regained his throne by force, the Ranas isolated Nepal from the rest of the world, ruling mostly by decree and severely persecuting any perceived infraction against their rule.

The majority of Nepalis at that time professed Hinduism. A minority, however, held to the tenets taught by Buddha. Over the years, these two religions intermingled to create a strange mix. The Ranas tolerated this mix, but new ideas were not. Christianity of the occasional traveler who reached Nepal's borders was not welcomed. Except for rare occasions, such travelers would be denied entry. After King Tribhuvan regained power, he opened the borders to commerce. But to Christianity, his kingdom remained closed.

Under the Ranas, very few were allowed to leave the country. Those who did, were rarely allowed back to live a life unmolested. Among those who did, were the famous Gurkha regiments, originally made up of young men from the Gorkha district of central Nepal. Famous for their bravery and discipline, these served valiantly in several wars under British commanders. Upon returning, they would bring back stories and news of the rest of the world. After the kingdom was restored, the Gurkhas remained as the primary collectors of foreign ideas and news.

One soldier, Prem Predhan, accepted Jesus Christ and returned to tell the Good News. His influence, magnified by his position in a Gurkha regiment, went unchecked for awhile. Soon, however, the coexisting alliance of Hindus and Buddhist became threatened by this upstart religion which seemed to spread like the monsoons. Its perceived peril was however not seasonal like the rains. More and more Nepalis of all ethnic groups embraced the freedom offered by Christ.

The ruling councils of the new royal government, or panchayats as they were called, felt threatened. Repression far greater than that exercised by the Rana family was soon felt by the new Christians. The law stated that no one was allowed to change their religion and no one was allowed to influence another to change his or her religion. The King's panchayats forced Prem Predhan and his converts into a series of jail terms. Fourteen jail terms and one confinement in an insane asylum resulted in the formation of fifteen new Churches as Prem witnessed to his cell mates. Subsequently he was released. Because Nepal's laws at the time stated that all children should be of the same religion as their parents, Prem and his wife began adopting. This resulted in another sixty year jail term but was overturned by the King when he learned of Prem's social work with Nepali children. Nevertheless, Nepal's prisons detained Christians in the same manner well into the early 1990's.

During their rule, the Ranas erected a series of palaces. I was now sitting on the outside patio of one of these. Today, it was called, 'Mike's Breakfast'. No longer are the Ranas served delicacies by servants. An American expatriate now serves omelets, quiche and fried eggs to a mostly western clientel.

Across from me sat one who had suffered at the hands of the panchayats. She had been detained in cold prison cells and denied reentry along Nepal's northern borders despite her possession of a valid visa. She had been ridiculed, spit upon, and belittled. The government of King Birendra Shah, who had come to power in 1972, had been less than hospitable towards her. Yet she had taken into her own home the most poor and destitute Nepalis and refugee Tibetans. She had collected the orphans and had fed them. She gathered unto her the sick and nursed them, even to her own detriment. On at least one occasion that I know of, she had spent the night coughing blood and gasping for oxygen from bacteria she had contracted from those she had assisted. She had given unto the fathers and husbands money that she had so desperately needed. In short, over the past sixteen years she had scraped the filthy streets of Kathmandu for outcasts, those forgotten by the rest of society, and had provided for them.

It was therefore fitting that she now sat on Ranas' patio awaiting breakfast. She served the people, albeit, poor ones. It was now time for her to be served; although she deserved much more than eggs and toast.

"How is the work?" I had asked after cursory greetings. She had already introduced me to Debra, sitting on her left. Debra had come to help Pam temporarily after hearing her speak at a conference in Australia.

"We had to move. We had simply outgrown our old house where you visited a few months ago." I remembered the house and the number of people at that time. I wondered then how so many could live under such cramped conditions. But her move was not too surprising. She constantly combed the streets for others in need.

"We now live in a larger house just outside of town, but still close to Bodha." She was referring to Bodhnath, the Buddhist stupa near her Church. Her love was for the Tibetan people, many of whom would pilgrimage to this stupa, rounding it relentlessly, turning the prayer wheels or writing prayers on flags. Several times I had been with her as she stopped to share Christ in Tibetan to a weary pilgrim at the base of the stupa. God had anointed her for that purpose.

"Our problem, however, is the well," Pam continued. "For months we had no water. The landlord had insisted that the well was a working one prior to our moving in. But once in, we had no water. As you know, water is important here in this dust and grime, especially with twenty-four orphans to care for, in addition to the occasional visitor."

The 'occasional visitor', I knew, represented those she had rescued from the street to feed and nurse back to health. They were neither 'occasional' nor 'visitors' since there was a steady stream of them and many stayed for weeks, if not indefinitely.

"How long have you had this problem?" I asked for clarification.

"Well, 'had' is the correct terminology," she replied, "Because the well now has water. But we had the problem for about three months."

I suppose she could read my surprised expression on my face because she quickly added, "Yes, Dr. Price, for three months we cared for our twenty-four children without water. During this time, we had a problem with lice. All of us itched ourselves raw until finally, I had enough."

"What did you do?" I asked. I guessed that she had forced the landlord to dig a deeper well.

"We prayed."

"You didn't dig deeper?"

"Nope. I finally was so frustrated that I gathered all the children plus my helpers and marched up to the well. Once there, I had them hold hands and I cried out to God. I told God that I was trying to care for these orphans of the street as He had instructed me and I did not feel like we should have to go without water anymore. Then I opened my eyes and commanded the well to produce water, just like Moses did to the rocks in the desert."

"What happened?"

"I instructed one of the older children to drop the bucket and get water. And to my surprise, the bucket came back up full of water. So we dropped it again and it was full a second time. That day we had enough water for all our needs."

I could see the excitement on her face.

"But that's not all," she added. "The next day, the older boys I had sent to fetch the water came back to report that the well was dry. So I marched everyone back up there, cried out to God, and again commanded the well in Jesus' name to produce water. And it did. So now, everyday, we pray and get water. It has not failed us! But if we do not pray, the well is dry."

"Our neighbors, who live down the hill from us saw that we had water. They, too, had no water in their wells. But since we, who lived higher than they, were now getting water, they assumed that their wells would also produce. However, their wells remain dry. They have now been digging for three weeks. Still, they have no water. So they asked me what I did and I told them exactly as I have just told you."

With a big smile, she said, "It has been a great testimony to those Hindus and Buddhists. It never fails that after I tell them, their eyes are as big as Bodha's." Again she was referring to the Buddhist stupa which has large eyes painted on one side.

"Anything new at the Church?" I asked.

"Absolutely!" Her exclamation startled the man and woman at the next table. Likely, they were from the diplomatic corps, looking very much like Americans. Mike's Breakfast was one of the few restaurants in Kathmandu that had been given the stamp of approval by the American Embassy (officials from the American Embassy test the food and water in local restaurants to determine the safety of such). They soon returned to their conversation and newspaper. Nevertheless, I am sure that their ears were still as attentive as mine to Pam's words. Debra also noticed them and gave me a half smile when she turned in my direction. Pam was oblivious to them as she was intent upon her story.

"The Church is overflowing!" Pam continued. "It is packed out every service. So we have bought land for a new building and now have regular outreaches into the surrounding villages. Since the democracy movement a few years ago, more and more Nepalis have become extremely hungry for the Gospel."

"For instance, a man from a distant village heard about our Church and therefore came for a visit. Although he did not accept Christ, he took some of our literature back to his village. Ten members of that village, after reading the literature, asked him how to be saved. Since he did not know, he brought them down to our Church. All got saved. They are now waiting for someone to come teach them more about Jesus in their own village. They have already bought the land for a new Church building!"

"A woman from another village heard about the Christians in Kathmandu. She therefore came down to the church for prayer because her child was dying. The Church prayed. Upon returning to her village, she found the child totally healed!"

By now, the man and woman at the next table had placed their papers to one side. They were no longer talking. Maybe it was my imagination but perhaps they, too, were intent upon Pam's words.

After my expressions of awe, she continued. "In Hetauda Sikrani, yet another village, over 300 were initially interested in the Gospel. But then intense persecution broke out. The Pastor and several members were beaten up severely. However, we at the 'mother' church began to intercede via prayer and fasting. The result was that the local lama that was behind much of the persecution was healed by the power of God. The beatings, of course, stopped immediately. Now, they have 25 baptized believers with 30 attending regularly."

"The village of Lanosangu now has 100 believers. Some walk four hours followed by a 1 hour bus ride to get to the services there. God has healed many. One boy who could not walk ran out of the Church after he was healed."

"What about the medical training of your workers?" I asked. "Did it make any difference?"

"Oh, yes indeed!" she exclaimed. "After you taught us the basics, we sent several teams and now there is interest in the Kothang district, Solu Khumbu, Dolpo and even Okhladunga district. These were very hard places for us before we began dispensing the medicines as you taught us. But now, not only do they want the medicines, but they also are receptive to the Gospel message."

"We have only one problem."

"What's that?" I asked.

"We need more workers.... The harvest is truly ripe. We've had pleas from four additional villages that I have not told you about. But until we get more help, we cannot go. Please pray the lord of the harvest to send forth laborers."

Later in the day, I headed across town. Neil met me at the Church, as he did at the airport earlier in the week. He and I would talk later about establishing medical clinics up in the mountain villages of Nepal. We would meet with several from India, Nepal, and even Bhutan who were interested in this very thing. I hoped to support these with medicines and finances to take the Gospel and healing to those living in the high and very dark places: where abides spiritual wickedness in high places.

The conference was hosted by Neil and his brothers. The three of them, Neil, Sandy, and Guine, were born in Goa, the Portuguese colony on India's west coast. Because of financial difficulties after the death of their mother, they were separated at an early age. Individually, they were forced to forge their way in life, each raised in a different orphanage. One by one, they came to know Christ as Savior. Miraculously, they ultimately found each other again and formed a nonprofit organization to assist local Pastors and Evangelists. It began right here in Nepal but soon spread to surrounding countries including Thailand, China, India, Bhutan, and others. Because of their background, they also have established Christian orphanages, one located in Kathmandu. Most of those attending the conference were in some way, completely or partially, financially supported by the brothers' efforts.

As I walked across the churchyard, lunch was just being served. Piles of rice, curried vegetables and the usual meat of unknown origin were being hungrily devoured in Indian fashion; no utensils except a plate and a right hand. Those hands were shoveling in this mixture as if there were no tomorrow. Around towards the back of the Church was the large cooking pot, attended by a few Nepali women feeding wood to the fire below. Smells of curry pierced the air and stung my eyes. Those from the Indian subcontinent have always explained that curry's ability to cause sweating and watery eyes was directly proportional to its desirability.

Suddenly, a plate with heaping portions was shoved my way. I looked down to see steaming curry. Almost instantaneously, my forehead beaded sweat and my eyes burned with tears. My throat tightened, obviously in efforts to spare my stomach lining. I looked around desperately for some bottled water, only to see the grinning faces of Nepalis and Indians.

Someone said, "The doctor loves curry. Look at his plate!" Everyone soon concurred and set their plates aside to witness my first bite. My hand hesitated and shook, also apparently allied with my stomach. Slowly, however, a portion was prepared. I swallowed. My throat grudgingly accepted. My stomach churned.

Seconds seemed like hours. Yet I survived. Those around me, satisfied that I had passed the test, hungrily returned to their meals. Fortunately, my hand had deftly increased the portion of rice and limited the curry. The blander rice, even with the occasional rocks, was always a lifesaver.

After lunch, I found myself at the pulpit presenting my testimony to the pastors. The church was built in the shape of a cross. Therefore, I spoke to those seated cross-legged to my right, to my left, and directly in front of me. Towards the middle of my time, a hindu holy man wandered in towards the back. His hair was unkempt, uncut and partially tied in a bun. His forehead shone red with evidence of recent hindu worship. He wore a faded and grimy dhoti. Those in the back, ushered him to a seat. He sat attentively until I finished. Then he left as he came, without a word.

I believe the Holy Ghost brought him to hear the Word of God in my testimony. This Word, accompanied by the blood of the Lamb, will overcome the devil. I look forward to the day when this man will clearly see God's authority.

I am sure that Neil and his brothers will see to it.

14 MARCH

At 8:00AM, her bus arrived. I had been waiting in the morning chill on the lawn just outside the hotel lobby. While waiting, I tried to start a conversation with the gardener who was manicuring the lawn with a pair of scissors. As is common to Asians, he squatted as he worked. Rather than assuming an upright position upon cropping the grass within his reach, he would contort his body to move to the next spot. Looking at him work prompted me to give forth a stretch to loosen my stiff back.

We had talked briefly about the growing problem of smog in the Kathmandu valley when Pam's bus arrived, belching black diesel smoke, and piercing the morning calm with a grumbling engine and exhausted shocks. Likely, those shocks had worn out long ago. Even in Kathmandu the roads were more potholes than pavement. Whereas the mountain roads were just potholes. As for the smog problem, this smoke belching machine was just one of the thousands that plied the valley's thoroughfares. No wonder the white slopes of the surrounding himalayas could rarely be seen from the valley anymore.

Pam wasn't on board. Instead, she had sent her driver to fetch me. As usual, her driver was accompanied by a friend, who also brought along a few other friends. I would soon realize that the one friend's job was to pound on the side of the vehicle with his flat palm on different occasions. There must have been some code to the pounding because the driver seemed to respond in different ways dependent upon the intensity and frequency of the pounding. The friends had no job. They were just along for the ride: except when I looked at them, they would immediately stop what they were doing to smile toothy grins.

They had piled my bags on a vacant seat, and off we roared and squeaked. With every turn I was sure of the antiquity of the shocks. I wondered how we remained upright.

Soon, we were on the outer ring road which encircled the city. Our speed had increased to create quite a breeze through the open windows protected only by faded blue and flapping curtains. Outside, we passed stone and brick cottages. The surrounding golden fields lay apparently barren, yet ready for a new planting season which was only weeks away.

Our speed slowed and a left turn placed us on a dirt embankment. To my surprise, it turned into a road, which to my greater surprise, the driver was attempting to maneuver. We now moved at just a crawl, yet an off-balance one. Immediately, I realized our precarious condition as the vehicle lurched towards the fifty foot ravine to our left. The rains had washed away any gravel that may have protected the muddy roadbed. Vast holes were thereby created which in turn caused our sway and pitch. Everyone knew that a road such as this was not made for a vehicle of this size and shape: everyone except our driver.

My bags soon deposited themselves on the floor. They had simply given up any effort to hold on to their seat under these conditions. But I resisted, insisting on holding on to my place with both hands firmly clenched to the railing in front of me. My knuckles were white. My neck was red.

The engine strained. Gears grind. The friend occasionally beat the side of the bus. The ravine became deeper and closer as we ascended. My bags banged against the wall. I no longer sat but stood, grasping a handle above the window to my right. The railing before me was simply not enough.

Soon, however, the hurricane ride came to an end as the ground leveled off and gravel reappeared. Also appearing was a house surrounded by a stone wall. We came to a squeaking rest on the barren land a few meters away from the front door, just inside the walls.

I sat for a few minutes catching my breath and relaxing my muscles in the now idle bus. Dust of the journey just accomplished soon caught up to us and gently created a brown film on the seats. With one great sigh of relief, I extricated myself, and then turned my attention to my bags wedged beneath the opposite seat. Once they were safely back in place, I ventured down the steps to the gravel courtyard.

Immediately, they surrounded me, chattering away happily in their native Nepali. I, not understanding a word, looked around desperately for a familiar face, or at least one that spoke English. Some would venture close to me to briefly touch my pant legs, and then quickly draw back. Such action would create quite a reaction of glee from the crowd. The brave one would soon melt back into the surrounding mob and be welcomed as a conquering hero. Such it is for Nepali orphans. The excitement of the moment is a welcome diversion to the stark realities of life.

Pam was nowhere to be found. The only one who knew any English seemed to be the driver's friend who was now standing with his friends near the just vacated bus. I approached with my hoards of admirers following.

"Where's Pam?" I asked.

The response was a blank look of ignorance. I don't know why I expected anything different. It was if they were thinking, 'Pam who?'.

Meanwhile the children around me were getting braver by the second as more and more were probing my defenses. By now several were constantly brushing my legs amidst the giggles and laughter that surrounded us.

Suddenly, I heard an apparent sharp rebuke from the house. Immediately, the laughter stopped and the children scattered. I looked towards the source of this energy that had violated the laws of nature. After all, order had just been created out of disorder. Not to my surprise, it was a wiry woman with a voice as shrill as her expression. However, when she saw my gaze, her countenance changed into a bright smile, which only accentuated the wrinkles about her high cheek bones and narrow eyes.

She then spoke in Nepali to the driver's fiend. He then turned to me and said in heavily accented English, "She said Pam will soon return. She ran an errand."

I found a place next to the wall on the step. As I sat there, the brave ones slowly began to return. The other children soon followed. Again I was surrounded. This time, since I was at their level, I noticed their coughs and nasal drainage.

A three year old girl was closest to me. With her every breath, I could hear a rattle. A stream of pus flowed from her nose down to her mouth. I reached into my bag to find a penlight and stethoscope. My stethoscope amplified the rattle into a roar. The light revealed rivers of pus pushing down her pharynx.

"Get a piece of paper." I instructed. The driver's friend immediately spoke to the woman who hurried off to accomplish the task.

"What is her name?" I asked when she returned with paper and pencil in hand. The driver's friend served as interpreter, the woman as the secretary. "Just write it down," I added. After a pause to allow her time to write I continued, "Next to her name write down, 'amoxicillin 250 milligrams, one by mouth, three times a day'." I had remembered the bottles of medications that I had given Pam just yesterday. We would put them to use this very day.

Soon, the children gathered even closer. It was no longer a game of tag. Even they, at their young age, understood. The medicines could make them well again.

As I looked in the ears of the second patient, a boy of about nine, I temporarily thought about the possibility of my catching what he and his playmates had. Likely, they were teaming with <u>Streptococcus</u>, <u>Haemophilus</u>, <u>Klebsiella</u>, <u>Staphylococcus</u>, as well as other potentially deadly organisms. Then I recalled Pam mentioning yesterday that several of her children had tuberculosis, which is transmitted very easily via airborne droplet nuclei. In other words, tuberculosis could be spread not only via a cough, but also by simply talking. Just then, my thoughts were interrupted by the productive coughs of several close to me.

Then I looked into the deep brown eyes of the nine year old before me. The conjunctiva were red and injected, obviously infected. His skin on his cheeks was dry and parched. The corners of his mouth had cracks and fissures. When he opened his mouth, he too had pus on his pharynx, and his tonsils were beet red with pockets of infection percolating from them. The woman with the paper said something to him in Nepali which caused him to open the buttons of his threadbare shirt. Every rib was clearly visible. He had no subcutaneous tissue to spare. He had many reasons to be malnourished: tonsillitis, pharyngitis, sinusitis, bronchitis, possible tuberculosis, and probably worms. In addition, he had lost his parents; either through death or abandonment.

His welfare was my responsibility, irregardless of my risk. I would hope that if my children were in a similar circumstance, God would send someone to help. For him and his friends, God had sent me.

By the time Pam came walking up the path, we had a long list with 24 names. Each little boy and girl would receive at least one type of medicine, most would receive several.

"I am so sorry," Pam began as she showed me in to her front room. We both deposited our shoes near the doorway as per Nepali custom. "I had to get up early to run an errand."

"It's not a problem," I answered. I was just a bit surprised she did not have another new orphan in tow. Pam's heart could leave no one begging on the streets. She always had room for one more at the dinner table, or one more mat for someone to sleep on. She had told me once that an American pastor said she lived 'a life on the edge'. She wanted to know what that expression meant, as she sometimes had problems with American slang. I had told her that 'living on the edge' is exactly what she does.

She offered a lukewarm cup of tea and then turned to give instructions in Nepali to her helper. The woman who had written down all the names and had created order out of disorder set the drink before me.

As she approached the table, I could see her facial features much more clearly. Her face was like leather; beaten by the himalayan winds and burned by the unfiltered ultraviolet rays of lofty elevations. Pterygion covered her eyes: again the result of unchecked ultraviolet rays. I thought she was in her fifties. Imagine my surprise when I learned she was but in her early thirties!

She spoke a few Nepali words to Pam. Pam turned, "She wants to know when you will return to give more medical training."

I looked at her again. I was a bit embarrassed that I had not recognized her. Yet I did remember when we had first met. It was in December 1990 in a church that was nothing like those in America. There were no wood-paneled walls, plush carpeted floors or stained glass windows. The light was dim; a sixty watt bulb hung precariously from the clay tile roof. I had followed the wiring up through the rafters and down the brick wall to the switch. The walls were simple brick, nothing more. Occasionally, the mortar between the bricks had eroded away, or perhaps been eaten by the many rats I had earlier seen in the street. The floor was covered with wool carpets; each with different faded colored designs of the typical tibetan coins in their centers. As I removed my boots I wondered how black my white socks would be by the end of the evening.

The group of Nepali pastors and evangelists had gathered towards the front of the room, opposite from where I was standing. She was among them.

That night we commenced our teaching of these Christians. We reviewed the medical problems so common among the himalayan villages. Our home church, Lakewood (Houston, Texas) had provided funds to purchase medical supplies. My wife, young son and Justin, Lakewood's administrator, had packaged these supplies earlier in the day into medical kits. Now it was time to present these kits to these newly trained health care workers. They were willing to go up into the mountain villages and treat the sick who previously had little access to medical care. I saw her reach for her bag of medicines and clutch it tightly.

We prayed for God's protection in Jesus' Name. I did not know if I would ever see any of them again in this life. Some were going to places where Christians had previously been persecuted very severely and even stoned. I hoped the medical kits would prevent such treatment. But I wasn't sure.

She left with her bag. I subsequently returned to Houston.

Often, in my comfortable surroundings in Houston, I wondered about her and her co-workers. I wondered if the medicines actually made it to those in need; if the stonings persisted.

She spoke to Pam in her native Nepali. Pam turned to me, "She wants to learn more about treating the sick."

As I heard the translation I examined her even more keenly. I saw her bare feet, cracked and calloused. Her toenails were short and thick. Layers of dried mud adhered to the webs of her toes like cement.

"Several months ago", Pam began, " shortly after you instructed the pastors, we sent them out with the medical kits. She of course, was one of those. Because of her concern for her native village, she first went there."

The morning sun had now begun to bear down upon the cinder block house. Poor ventilation added to the radiating heat. Yet my attention was now intently upon Pam.

Again the woman spoke. After several interchanges between Pam and the woman, I asked, "What did she say?"

"She was telling me about her trip to her home village. Let me fill you in. She first took public transportation as far as she could go."

As she was speaking I imagined what such transportation was like. I had seen and experienced bus rides through the mountain roads of Nepal. Actually, they are better termed gravel trails. Frequent land-slides cause even more rudimentary segments. The jostling and turning within the bus which are usually overloaded not only with other Nepalis but also with produce and various animals must have been extremely hard on her.

"Then she began a trek of many weeks. She was forced to cross the roaring mountain rivers 32 times; sometimes via rope bridge, at other times by cable (a large hemp rope with a pulley and basket). But most of the time she waded across. Of course when she waded she was forced to place the medicines and Christian literature on her head. It was late in the spring so she didn't bring any shoes but she ran into unexpected snow."

"You mean she trekked in snow barefoot?"

"Exactly! At times it was up to her calves. She was also forced to take nose-to-heel inclines"

"What's that?"

"Nose-to-heel? That means her nose was at the heels of the one in front of her on the incline as she climbed. It was also necessary for her to climb along cliffs with five to six inch ledges as trails. She often looked down and saw human skeletons where those who had gone before had fallen. Because of the repeated trauma of her feet against the rocks and cliffs she lost all the toenails from one foot."

I again glanced down at her feet. I now had a new appreciation for her mangled toenails.

The missionary continued, "One night she slept in a cave. When she awoke the next morning she discovered she was lying beside some human skeletons."

"Finally she arrived at her home village. People were so hungry for the Gospel they would constantly awaken her at night to hear more. It was common that after a long day of teaching, someone would bang at her door at 2:00AM. She stayed several days but then needed to get back to Kathmandu. As she left they were pleading for her to stay longer or send someone else to their village to teach about Jesus."

"Were the medicines of any benefit?" I asked.

"Absolutely! Many received treatment for worms, skin infections, diarrhea, bronchitis and sinusitis as you instructed. But more importantly, when the medicines ran out, the villagers would go and buy similar medicines at the pharmacy and bring them back to her."

"Why did they do that?"

"Because the villagers said that without prayer in the Name of Jesus, these very same medicines would not work! Only when this woman prayed as she gave the medicines would the sickness leave. This is especially important because we had gone to this village before without medicines, and they had no interest in any of our Gospel literature. In fact, these very same villagers had driven us out with sticks and stones!"

Later that day with bags in hand, I found myself walking across the tarmac to Thai Airways flight 312 bound for Bangkok. As I reached the plane I turned for one more view of the valley. The lone runway was several hundred feet above the surrounding countryside. All of Kathmandu valley could be seen from my vantage point. I could see Bodhnath, the buddhist stupa where I had seen Tibetan pilgrims walking around in a clockwise direction, dutifully spinning prayer wheels and chanting. Although from this distance I could not see them, Buddhists monks with their entourage of young disciples would be up on the stupa and prayer flags would be waving uselessly in the breeze.

In another direction I could see Pashupatinath, the Hindu temple and holy burial grounds. I will never forget the "holy men" in their loin cloths with their glassy-eyed western followers (as if they were drugged), and the wails of a family of a recently departed soul. The stench of death from the funeral pyres on the banks of the Bagmati River was as thick as the spirit of hopelessness in that place. Downriver from the funeral pyres a devotee would be bathing and drinking the death stained waters. Rhesus monkeys, with their menacing, piercing eyes, would be everywhere.

Then I looked towards the city. I remembered the orphans in their tattered rags and the physically deformed beggars pleading so desperately on the streets. Refuse would be littered everywhere, whereas faces would be lined with the miseries and worries of life. Unbelievable burdens would be piled on the backs of frail women, children would be playing barefoot in the open sewers, and men would be squandering hard-earned money to buy a chicken for sacrifice to a stone-cold, dead god. The travel brochures described Nepalis as happy-go-lucky. But I witnessed the truth; average lifespan 47, per capita income $160, alarmingly high infant mortality, and only one doctor for every 20,254 people. In short, sickness abounds both physically and spiritually.

I turned towards the airbus and boarded. Soon I was in my seat and the plane was roaring down the runway. As we catapulted from the earth, I looked out the window towards the terraced himalayan mountains; truly a peaceful and quaint site. Occasional a brick cottage arose from the rice and barley fields.

NEPAL — MARCH 1992

Mountain streams pierced the valleys and rugged trails marked the slopes. In the distance the high elevations of Mt. Everest, Annapurna, and K2 pointed towards heaven. Yet I knew that the seemingly peaceful existence imagined from the airplane and viewed from a distance did not correlate with the realities of life up close in that rugged heathen land.

Then I remembered the woman with the weather-beaten face, scarred eyes, and cracked and calloused feet with mangled toenails. Materially, she had little. But it was she who had delivered a pearl of great price to those in a distant mountain village.

They will be forever grateful.

But there are hundreds, perhaps thousands, of villages that have not even heard the name of Jesus, much less what He has done for them. They do not know about the free gift that will deliver them from their present darkness. They remain in misery and torment. Their diseases consume them. Spiritual wickedness destroys them.

She was willing to lose a few toenails. I must be willing to do the same.

Colombo

Batticaloa

SRI LANKA APRIL 1993

11 APRIL

"Doctor, can you help me and my friends?"

My gaze turned towards the young man's query. He was extremely thin, almost to the point of emaciation. As he spoke it was as if he were struggling for each word and battling for every breath. He had no might.

This gaunt young man truly was near faint and was clearly weary. He was quite close to falling. His brown skin beaded with perspiration, especially across his furrowed brow. His bloodshot eyes were filled with despair.

With his very last milligram of energy he had made his way to me. I had positioned my small table in the shade of a palm tree where I was examining the infirm. He definitely fit in with the rest. All appeared ill. All were certainly needful of our humanitarian aid. But deliverance from spiritual darkness was their biggest need. That deliverance is what he sought.

"Doctor, can you help me and my friends?" he had said. And then he slowly explained, "You see, we are just hopeless heroin addicts."

It was with these words that I clearly saw him. He had obviously made some bad decisions to bring him to his addiction. Probably others had seen him as a dirty, unkempt addict; living in the sewer gutters of life. But God's compassion made me see him as somebody's little boy: a thin emaciated child that needed my help. He likely had tried every other conceivable method to free himself from his cursed addiction; but to no avail. He had come to the very end of his frayed rope. It was for him, and his two boyish companions, one hindu and one buddhist, that I had come.

"I'm sorry," I began, "I don't have any medicines for you." His head immediately dropped. Undoubtedly, he had seen me treat the others with medications that we had brought for their specific ailments. Now his hope for a cure was temporarily crushed. The late afternoon sun reflected off the tears that had suddenly welled up in his eyes.

"But I have something even better!" I continued. Through his unblotted tears I could see his bewilderment.

"Follow me." I instructed.

With that I turned to Princely, my interpreter. "Let's go." Princely and the three boys followed me through the crowd of those yet to be examined and those waiting for their prescriptions. Before the day was over, I would treat 115 patients. All would receive free examinations and medications without cost. They would also receive prayer. Thirty would accept Jesus as Savior for the first time.

My shirt stuck to my back. Colombo's sweltering afternoon heat, radiating off the surrounding asphalt and cinder block buildings, was unrelenting. Faint breezes were few and far between. As I made my way through the warm bodies, I marveled at how the Sri Lankans always appeared so cool, seemingly unaffected by the equatorial heat. At seven degrees north latitude, Colombo was always hot.

Finally I delivered the addicts for prayer. Hands were laid upon them. Almost immediately, the Holy Ghost fell. Tears of despair had turned to shouts of joy as they began speaking in a heavenly language to their Redeemer.

It was Easter Sunday. For these three boys, the resurrection had come.

12 APRIL

By his dress, he was obviously Muslim. His blue cap was perched atop a graying head which extended uninterrupted to a curly beard. His voluminous tunic was also blue. Next to him, his wife sweltered beneath a dark blue scarf which concealed her head, neck and hair. They must have been hot, yet not a drop of perspiration dampened them.

They were waiting conspicuously for my examination in folded chairs just opposite the empty one reserved for me. Their family surrounded them attending to every whim or desire. As it turned out, she was in no acute distress. However, he was quite a different matter. He had hypertension and diabetes with the resulting coronary artery disease. Because of such, he was also in mild congestive heart failure. I was, of course, expected to give him a pill or two to make him into a new man. In the eyes of many in the developing world, American doctors and American medication conjured up even magical connotations. Yet that day I would have no magic for him.

It was a shock to see him or anyone like him. The clinic had been sponsored as a Christian event; an event that Muslims usually do not frequent. But he was sick and needed my help. Indeed I would help him: not to the extent that I would have liked. My expert medical opinion dictated acute hospitalization for his woes. Yet hospitalization, even in Colombo, was not an option. "How long have you had diabetes?" I asked him directly. He shifted his weight and with a slight turn of his head directed my attention to his son just behind him.

His son answered, "For many years. But recently, he has had much troubles, as we discussed earlier."

I had met his son for the first time a few days previously in his small second floor shop. Larry had taken me to him. At the time, I thought the exact timing of our visit was less than opportune. It was Saturday, holy day. Once close to the mosque, our driver slowed to a crawl. Even though the street was wide, departing worshippers occupied every square inch. Bearded men were dressed in white from head to toe; even white caps adorned every head. All peered menacingly through the taxi windows. I knew that some zealot muslims taught that those such as myself were no more than infidels and deserved quick death. My hope was that the sermon that day was on a different passage of scripture.

Within this sea of humanity we had come to a stop. "Let's go." Larry had said. I remember asking with a bit of incredibility in my voice, "You mean we're getting out?" I was wondering if the menacing stares would evolve into something more, like a riot with us in the middle. But I soon found myself making my way on foot, in the midst of the mob in white, towards a row of shops. Fortunately, we actually had stopped close to the curb so my jaunt through the white gauntlet was only a short walk. The sidewalk, elevated several feet above street level, brought us to the row of shops. As is typical of the developing world, these were simple one room garage style structures, with one wall completely open to the street. Wares of various types spilled out onto the sidewalk, where potential customers in small groups haggled prices with the merchants. But rather than enter one of these, a small doorway appeared behind the meandering stares, haggling customers and weary merchants. We entered this doorway between two shops single-file.

A narrow passageway with a wet floor brought us to an enclosed courtyard. Bright sunlight filtered down in distinct beams between the wooden rafters and broken tile above. A small dilapidated stairway was our next hurdle which we traversed with much creaking. Once on the second floor balcony, we were beckoned into a small room lined with glass shelves. A similarly glass enclosed counter met us and folding chairs were brought out for our comfort.

A Tamil Christian, a converted Muslim, had brought Larry and myself to this place. He wanted us to meet his very good friend, the owner of this shop. Soon plastic containers were deposited on the countertop. The lids were removed to reveal rows of dirty and faded envelopes. To my surprise, each of these contained hundreds of sparkling sapphires.

In the midst of the attempted sale I was identified as a physician and the shop owner was told of our free clinic. It was then when he first told me of his father's ailments.

"Well bring him to the clinic!" I had said.

So I had known a little of the patient sitting before me well before I had actually seen him. My exam revealed the edema of congestive heart failure, the shiny skin of peripheral vascular disease, and the scars of previous diabetic ulcers. He had obviously been fortunate for these previous ulcers to heal. I decided to do my best to prevent future infections.

"I have three medications for you." I began. "One for your diabetes, another to decrease the swelling, and another to improve blood flow to your legs." I could only hope that they would be taken correctly. Princely, I trusted, would explain every detail in their native Tamil.

Suddenly, from near the pharmacy, a mother's cries could be heard above the surrounding din. All others stopped what they were doing as this mother continued her wailing. All attention was now upon her.

Soon Larry, who had gone to investigate, returned to us with a report. I had assumed she was in pain and needed my attention. "...Not so." Larry had said after I voiced my concern. "She's screaming for joy because her previously deaf and dumb child had begun to hear and speak."

The muslim at my side and his son also heard Larry's report. After whispering to his father, he turned to me. "Doctor? Will you also pray to Jesus for us?"

13 APRIL

The road had narrowed and the vegetation on each side had been cleared and burned. For a hundred yards on each side of the highway nothing taller than a twig was allowed. The ruling Buddhist Sinhala army was doing their very best. Nevertheless, civil war was far from won here in the Eastern Province. Beyond the twigs and in the midst of the dense tropical vegetation lurked the dreaded Liberation Tigers of Tamil Ealam.

At night they would strike; usually with uncanny precision. The result would be death of Sinhalese army personnel. Their methods often included TNT, either loaded onto stolen vehicles or strapped to their own bodies. In a kamikaze fashion, they would indiscriminately kill. However, reprisal would be swift. Anyone of the local Tamils could be looked upon with suspicion, and killed with a vengeance on the spot, many times with nothing more than sharpened machetes and without a trial. The New York Times had reported the massacre of innocent farmers and laborers who had simply been at the wrong place at the wrong time. Since 1983, when the uprising began, over 20,000 had died.

But the local populace is not only subject to atrocities at the hand of the Sri lankan army. The Tamil Tigers also demand obeisance and any suspicion of sympathy with the government results in severe punishment if not loss of life. In Batticaloa and surrounding villages, it was a subjugated people of two opposing unsympathetic, hate filled masters, one by day, the other by night.

Up ahead I spotted the first of many detours. As we approached, I could distinguish earthen embankments protecting a small army camp of thatch roofs and crude wooden walls. A lone tall tree stood at one end. In it, a sentry was perched scanning the surrounding countryside with field glasses.

We turned into the dusty detour. Billowing clouds of red dust trailed us as we bounced amongst the potholes. So did the eyes of several soldiers behind raised guns pointed in our direction. Heavy artillery also was directed toward us as we slowly encircled the camp. Finally, we were all relieved to reach the road once again. It was surprising that the narrow rocky road that previously had seemed so rough, now felt like glass.

We were to endure several more detours before our final destination. Nightfall was rapidly approaching. With it would be the curfew; the time after which all moving vehicles would be assumed to be the enemy by each side. Thereby lay our concern.

Our original timetable had us already safely in the resthouse at Batticaloa.

But both the van and driver were hard to come by once our final destination was revealed. No one was too anxious to risk life or vehicle in the war zone. Therefore, our departure from Colombo was delayed way past noon. En route, our driver stopped at a hindu shrine to pray for protection. Over the next few days he would learn of the true Protector.

Larry's ministry had been registered within Sri Lanka as a bonafide humanitarian aid organization. One of his board members, P. Balan, a Colombo businessman, had exerted his influence to acquire the van and driver, as well as entry permits for the war zone. Travel to the Eastern Province was strictly restricted.

Jim sat quietly beside me. He had traveled with Frank, a trained EMT, and their Pastor, Robert Dowdy, all the way from Galveston. Behind Jim and I sat Bob, a rancher from Marquez, Texas, and another Pastor from Portland, Texas. Finally, Michael, who had traveled via Royal Jordanian Airways from Dublin, Ireland and Hans, a Swede, completed the group of westerners within the van. They had all helped in various capacities in the Colombo medical clinics. They would do the same in the days ahead in the war zone. Long ago the hospital in Valechenai had been abandoned. Thus, the medical needs of the province had gone unmet for years.

The van slowed for yet another checkpoint. This time, Manuel, who was sitting next to the driver, got out to approach the guardhouse on foot. Manuel had at one time held a very good position in Australia. But God had led him back to the country of his birth. When he advised his employers in Perth of his decision, they offered him a significant salary increase. Nevertheless, he refused. Because he is an ethnic Tamil, he has taken many risks to minister Jesus in the war zone.

Through the dirty windshield, we could see Manuel discussing our purpose to several guards shouldering automatic weapons. Meanwhile, another guard approached the van. As he came closer, we could see he was very young, perhaps still in his teens. His eyes were bloodshot and his face lined with fatigue. I wondered whether his forlorn appearance was due to lack of sleep or an abundance of alcohol, or both. He nervously fingered the trigger on his weapon which he held securely with both hands and pointed in our direction.

Inside the van, all was quiet.

Manuel was walking back slowly with two armed soldiers. One of them waved a command to the lone soldier already beside the van. Immediately, he shouldered his firearm, slid open the side door and began opening our bags. One of the soldiers with Manuel soon joined in, while the other stood to the side.

SRI LANKA — APRIL 1993

Meanwhile, time passed and the sun slid rapidly towards the horizon.

Dusk was upon us when we finally were allowed to pass. The sun had slid beneath the hill country and darkness would be only minutes away. All remained silent as the motor hummed with the rising speed. We all recognized that the many miles ahead of us would be taken in total darkness in violation of the Sinhala imposed curfew. As the last traces of sunlight were being swallowed by night, we also wondered whether the eyes of the dreaded Tamil Tigers were even now stalking our path.

We passed a bombed out and now abandoned army base. The walls were pock-marked with bullet holes and the surrounding area was riddled with mortar craters. Not too far further we surveyed the remains of a burned car body. Someone asked, "Is that also the result of a Tamil attack?"

Manuel answered from his seat in the front which we in the back could not quite make out. But those closer to him relayed his message. "No. The owner of the car destroyed it himself. He didn't want to take the risk of being forced to let the Tigers use it and then being accused by the Sinhalese of being a rebel sympathizer, or vise versa."

It was pitch black as we raced south towards Batticoloa. The driver had illuminated the dome lights so all who may be observing could see the white skin of westerners, and not army nor Tiger personnel.

Additional army checkpoints lay ahead. Our bags again would be scrutinized. Between checkpoints, we all rode in silence. But silent prayers could be heard above the drone of the engine.

Suddenly we braked hard and came to a stop in the middle of the highway. The driver then immediately shifted into reverse and backed quickly several feet. The doors of the van were forced open to reveal several dark faces.

Smiles developed. We had made it to Batticaloa. The faces were those of local Christians who had waved the driver to a stop. Our bags were soon carried into the brick rest house.

A few minutes later I lay on a split bamboo cot by the open window hoping for a breeze in the stifling heat. It's good to know that prayers, even silent ones, do not go unanswered.

Sleep came easy.

14 APRIL

"Three months ago his church building had been burned to the ground by militant hindus on this very spot. Now, as you can see, it has been resurrected!"

We were standing in front of a simple structure of bamboo and nipa. It had a three foot wall around it connected to the roof via wooden beams. The roof actually was a double roof, a smaller one sitting atop the larger like a hat. A small space between the roofs allowed for the hot air to escape thereby producing better ventilation for its occupants. Inside, the floor was earthen, covered with the feet of hundreds of worshippers.

Larry was explaining about Pastor T. C. Mahendran's church in Valechenai which stood on three acres of grassy and sandy soil. Across the street was the abandoned hospital. In the afternoon, we would conduct our very first medical clinic in the Church. The very same hindus that had stormed and burned the original Church three months previously would receive medical help there.

After lunch, under the shade of a bent tree, we talked with a thin man with bloodshot eyes and a twisted smile. He was a worshipper of the god, kali. Kali, I knew, required sacrifice on stone altars. In India of the mid 1800's, a British expeditionary force had to be dispatched into the hinterlands to eradicate worshippers of this pitiful god. Their crimes centered upon kali's requirement of human blood sacrifice of innocents.

"Come to my house!", he insisted over and over. His eyes would glaze over as if another being controlled him. Like a puppet, he continued to repeat himself. "...Come to my house and I will show you kali...."

Finally, someone said, "Come to Jesus. He will show you rest and peace!"

His eyes temporarily cleared. Larry motioned towards me and said, "The doctor here has something important to say to you."

"I was once a prisoner of pain, but Jesus set me free." I began. "You are a prisoner of kali. Let Jesus free you too."

Later, the church building was turned into a medical clinic. Many of the militant hindus, whose only other attendance in church was to burn it down, were drawn by the free medical exams and medications. They are now former hindus, children of the Most High God! Our hope is that the thin man under a bent tree will also be free: not by the sacrifice required by kali, but by the sacrifice of Christ's blood.

Evening had finally fallen. The oppressive sun was gone but the sweltering humidity had assured the continued sauna-like atmosphere. We had taken a short walk from the guest house in Batticaloa to the home of Pastor G.J.Joseph. Across the street from his home was a vacant lot, and beyond that were the fields.

"Because of my location on the outskirts of town, the Sri Lankan army has suspected me of being a Tiger sympathizer." Pastor Joseph was saying as he motioned to the fields. We were sitting in his living room on wooden straight back chairs. The door was open to the elements. Rotating fans redistributed the warm and stifling air.

"In fact, that field is the very one where sixteen farmers were hacked to death by machetes at the hands of this very same military."

"Were these sixteen guilty?" I asked.

"I don't think so." Was his reply. As he spoke, the shrill music of a hindu celebration down the street pierced the air. Loudspeakers, filled with static, broadcast a soprano's voice accompanied by a sitar. The decibels seemed to rise with each score. I could imagine how the revelers were stirring themselves into a frenzy; giving themselves over to their gods; prostrating themselves before stone idols. Then I wondered about our friend who had worshipped kali, and others like him. What hope was there for a people surrounded by war and spiritual forces that fed on their misery?

Perhaps it was a night like this when the radical hindus stormed and burned the Church in Valechenai. Doubtless they too had been at a drunken celebration; one that was fostered by their despair. Their minds, clouded by incense smoke, drugs, and their emotions, stirred by alcohol and demon forces, resulted in a night of destruction. This night, I hoped for a different end.

Overhead, clouds had obscured the moon and the stars. Low wattage streetlights did little to fight off the molasses-like night. For those down the street, it was indeed dark.

Pastor Joseph continued. "On eight different occasions my house was searched and I was forcibly taken to the army headquarters and accused of being a spy and gunrunner. I didn't know if I would ever see my family again. But on each occasion, God delivered me."

After a short pause, he added with a distinct smile, "I also took each occasion to preach the Gospel to the officers. One time, an officer accepted Jesus. A week later he was killed in a Tiger raid."

A meal of rice, fish and bananas soon followed. Afterwards, we again walked back to the guesthouse. The hindu celebration could still be heard through the static. A few dogs bellowed their displeasure as we walked past. The purr of a motorcycle pierced the air in the distance as it went through its gears.

I had especially felt the heat. It was good to again savor the tropical, albeit warm, breeze through the open window beside my cot. Slumber came quickly. The day had been a long one.

At 1:00 A.M. I heard the thunder. I was glad. Perhaps the accompanying rain would cool things down a bit. I would not learn until the following morning that the thunder was not to be accompanied by rain, only death.

The army base down the street had been hit by Tiger mortars.

15 APRIL

Frank and Bob set up their triage desk at the very front foyer of the Church. Jim and Michael were busy passing out prescriptions in a side room. I was examining and prescribing with Princely again at my side. He was fluent in both Tamil and Sinhala and was therefore as vital to me now as he was in Colombo.

We were in a building less than a hundred yards from a Sinhala military camp. It was really not built as a Church, but as a private home. Its wealthy owners, however, had abandoned it to flee the war. Pastor Jesusdassan and his wife had been using it as The Christian Family Church.

On many occasions, the radical hindus, who had a temple just across the street, had attempted to drive them away. Yet they had remained strong and steadfast. They had refused to move.

Today they stood to one side with tears. I would learn later that they had never seen so many in their house of worship. Some they had recognized as those who had threatened them on other nights. Today these very same had thanked them for sponsoring the clinic. Their emotions could not be checked.

"Ask him how long it has hurt." I asked Princely.

After a flurry of Tamil, Princely turned to me to report, "He says he has had pain in his mouth for greater than a year."

The thin man before me was dressed in a worn and faded dhoti and a similarly threadbare shirt, open at the collar. He was bare footed and his toenails were thickened from neglect. His beard was unkempt and graying. Bloodshot and piercing eyes pled for answers to his problems.

I expected to see swollen tonsils, or perhaps purulent sinus drainage on a reddened and raw pharynx. I had seen so many of these over the previous days. But he opened his mouth to reveal a purplish-red, fungating mass. It was strictly adherent to his tongue and occupied most, if not all, of his oral cavity. A closer look revealed a multitude of fistula tracts draining pus within this mass. His teeth were mostly gone. A few stubs were dark and surrounded by swollen gums.

Now I understood his long term pain. His cachectic state was no longer a mystery. He scarcely could drink much less eat. Up until that point, I had sweated through many exams. But none were as heartwrenching as the man before me. He desperately needed surgery to at least establish a diagnosis.

His eyes pleaded for help.

But I could offer nothing but a few medicines: some to relieve his pain, others to fight off infection.

"Tell him that he needs more than just these medicines. He needs to go to Colombo as soon as possible."

Princely translated my response which I knew would be a disappointment. As he turned, his eyes changed. I was his last hope. He doubtless had no financial means to go elsewhere. His eyes had lost the faint glimmer of hope and now were again filled with despair. Most likely he had a malignancy. Of course, it could be less serious. Only a biopsy would tell.

On his prescription, I scribbled in large letters, 'PRAYER FOR HEALING'. He shuffled with drooping shoulders to the pharmacy. Listlessly, he handed his prescription to Jim. After I examined a few more patients, I noticed Jim praying for him with the help of his interpreter. I wanted to go over and join in, yet the anxious faces of those still waiting prevented my departure.

It was taking me longer than I expected. I was sure that I had seen all those that were waiting but the line was ever bit as long as if I had seen no one. So I continued. When I had examined these, the line still remained. Maybe I was confused. But likely there was a simpler explanation. A little investigation on my part proved my suspicions. Late arrivals were being covertly added. Those who were registering patients didn't have the heart to turn anyone away. All seemed so desperate.

Finally, after 115 exams, both my back and the time dictated an end to the day's clinic. The van was loaded and ready. We must leave soon. Otherwise we would again risk nightfall and the onset of curfew. We did not want to be a target, especially after the mortar attack of the night previous.

Those who still waited were given some vitamins and sent away with a prayer. Many needs remained.

The driver slowly eased away from the Church. The Christians, new and old, waved with smiles and tears. One of them was the man with the mouth tumor. He too had a smile despite his pain. I believe God heard our prayers. We had examined and treated 425 in the past four days, of which 120 made decisions to follow Jesus. From appearances, he was numbered among the saved.

Pastor Jesusdassan and his wife also wore smiles. They had seen 50 accept Jesus as Lord that very day via the temporary medical clinic. At their side was Pastor Joseph. As he waved and smiled, I couldn't help but wonder if he again would be interrogated. I prayed silently for his protection. Pastor Mahendran also stood beaming. Not only had he gained the respect of his neighbors for hosting the clinic yesterday, but through the benevolence of Lakewood Church in Houston, I was able to provide a cement floor, as well as the money to purchase the land on which his Church stood.

Our driver also had a new smile. That very morning, before we left the guesthouse, he had accepted Jesus. He had seen with his own eyes the protecting power of the Most High God. He, too, wanted that blessed assurance. We backtracked through the war zone. Again we detoured around military encampments and underwent physical search. We passed buildings scarred by bullets and huge mortar craters. In Valechenai, we passed by the crumbling foundation of the old police station: all that remained after a Tiger had stolen a truck, loaded it with dynamite and killed himself and several policemen in his final act.

By sundown, we had cleared the final checkpoint to be well on our way back to the relative safety of civilized Colombo. On our way, we had passed two burned out villages, which I had assumed to be the work of the Tigers. Much to my surprise, the Tigers had nothing to do with either. One was a Muslim village. An angry Hindu mob had torched it. The other was a Hindu village. Its destruction was in retaliation for the first.

Hate does not originate with the Tigers, nor with the Sinhala. The devil manipulates as many as he can.

Again our route took us across the island, just skirting the tea plantations of the central highlands. Kandy was first to our west, then south, and finally to the east of us. This old city was famous for many things, including a buddhist stupa where legend has it that an actual tooth of buddha lay buried. This has some sort of significance to his followers.

The next day I would read in Colombo's daily newspaper another reference to this buddha. Sri Lanka's President Ranasinghe Premadasa had evidently made a state visit to India. While there, he had visited the site in Uttra Pradesh where buddha had passed away and his remains (excluding the tooth, I suppose) are kept for 'public veneration'. Later in the day, the president had visited several other religious sites, including a statue depicting the dying buddha reclining on his right side with face towards the west. The Sri Lankan buddhist monks traveling with the president had appealed to him to construct a golden railing around the statue for its protection. He agreed to attend to it once he returned to Sri Lanka.

He never did.

Less than two weeks later, while attending a lighthearted May Day celebration in the security of Colombo, President Premadasa was killed. An assassin had strapped dynamite to himself and rode his bicycle to where the President was greeting the crowd. Edward Gargan of the New York Times reported that television pictures showed bodies scattered on the pavement, along with bits of clothing, broken signboards, shards of glass and shoes of people who fled. The president's security force of several bodyguards could do nothing to prevent this massacre. They too, including many innocent people, lay dead and mangled on the hot street.

In the past few days, we gave testimony of a healing, delivering, and living Jesus. In the shadow of the valley of death, surrounded by mortar fire, demonic rituals and pestilence and devoid of any visible security, we were protected. Many were also healed of sickness and delivered from demonic oppression as a demonstration of His unchanging and ever present love.

However, President Premadasa had no protection even in the security of Colombo and all his bodyguards and despite the good thoughts of his followers. Buddha, whose tooth is an object of worship in Kandy, the one whom the president revered and worshipped, the one who sought enlightenment, the one who taught of nirvana (albeit both unattainable and undefinable), could not protect him. Whether or not his tooth actually lay in a Kandy stupa is irrelevant. The man called buddha is dead.

Jesus, however, the One who was once dead, is very much alive. He is alive forevermore. Only He holds the keys to all the questions of this life.

The dedication and sincerity of the Sri Lankan Christians (without whom our medical clinics would not have been possible) are examples of Jesus Christ's answer to the Sri Lankan tragedy; love truly can overcome hate.

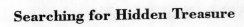

Varna

• Sofia

BULGARIA NOVEMBER 1993

Darkness had fallen. The small Russian-made Lada was struggling up and down the highway, hugging the mountainside and rumbling through occasional tunnels. We had departed Sofia at midday, six hours previously. Now on the final leg of our journey to the Black Sea port of Varna, we were in the middle of the Balkan Mountains.

When the headlights began to flicker off and on, I turned to my wife, Sue, who was sitting very close. Our suitcases were stacked on one half of the back seat. They were filled, not with clothes, but with precious medications for the destitute Bulgarians. With each curve and bump, they threatened to confiscate even more of the precious remaining space allowed for us. I considered asking Sue's thoughts concerning our situation, yet decided against it. Rather, we both sat in silence as all eyes strained into the darkness beyond the dim erratic headlights.

The rocky road ahead was quite precariously situated on the mountain's edge with a multitude of curves, dips and bends. Sue and I could only imagine what dangers lurked in the shadows. The constant rattle of the worn shocks and the intermittent knocking of the aged motor only reminded us of our precarious situation.

Suddenly, the struggling motor within the lada abruptly changed into a high-pitched whine. I remembered our stop just a few kilometers previously to fill the crankcase with oil. It was then when I first viewed the small engine. Now, with the motor's whine bouncing off my eardrums, I could only think of the lawnmower-sized engine that I was entrusting to take not only me, but also my wife, across the mafia-infested Balkans.

Minutes were like hours. The flicker of the headlights persisted. The black moonless night prevented our eyes from judging our altitude. It, however, did not prevent our imaginations from envisioning the precipice to which we inched closer with each bend in the road.

"Well," I thought, "At least we had some light. We weren't groping our way in total darkness."

As we entered a dark tunnel, the headlights went out for good.

4 NOV

Sofia was a dark, impersonal, polluted city. Bleak November clouds combined with black industrial smog created an atmosphere of foreboding. The communists had dreamed that this largely agrarian land could be transformed into an industrial showplace. Instead, the rustic land became polluted with disease and distrust. No one smiled. No one laughed. Even the children showed little emotion; neither tears nor laughter. Groups of men could be found standing in the morning chill, chain-smoking and speaking only in whispers. Decades of authoritarian rule muffled all outbursts that would draw attention. Attention, of course, would draw suspicion. Suspicion would lead to denouncement. Denouncement led to internal exile and a life of eternal refrigeration: never again to come in out of the cold.

Sue and I had arrived the evening before on the Balkan Bulgarian Airlines flight from Amsterdam via Vienna. In Amsterdam's Schipol Airport, we had felt fortunate to get non-smoking seats. Somewhere over Germany the inflight meal of cheese, cold sausage, and dry bread was delivered in a plastic carton. To wash this down, we were also served a plastic cup full of water which was so hard that we considered drinking it with a spoon. As Sue pointed out the green mold on her slice of cheese, smokers began to light up, including the man in the dark suit, black loafers, and white socks sitting across the aisle. To my consternation, smoke was everywhere. Obviously, I thought, the gentleman was disregarding the nonsmoking regulations in our area. My consternation dissolved into bewilderment when I ultimately realized he was not violating regulations. Truly, he was smoking in the smoking section which was located on the right side of the aircraft. We were sitting in the nonsmoking section limited to the left side of the aircraft.

Upon arrival at Sofia's international airport, we disembarked into a wintry night, made colder by the heavy mist that blanketed the tarmac and penetrated to the bone despite our heavy outer garments. Inside the crude terminal, masses of tired, smoking travelers, mostly in fashionless gray or black overcoats, shoved us various ways. Ultimately, however, our passports were stamped by an expressionless female agent and we were directed towards our bags. Nothing was said as another tired agent chalked our luggage and waved us through.

The only smiling faces in the small arrival hall were those of our Christian hosts, Nicolai and Blagovest (Blago). Soon we were on our way through the damp streets of Sofia in the back seat of a small Toyota; old but functional. A blur of tall poplar trees lined the streets enroute to the Moscow Park Hotel, our home for the next few days.

The Moscow Park Hotel was as hospitable as it sounds. We were forced to park on the street. The entry way was blocked by unoccupied late modeled black cars of Eastern European make. The doorman was, of course, not at the door, but inside watching the hotel's only television. He and his companions intently smoked the night away as they viewed the news dictated in a monotone but resonant male Bulgarian voice. I supposed that they had tuned the volume up so high because of their concern for the listening pleasure of their guests on the upper floors. Our arrival was needless to say of little consequence and precipitated not even a glance.

The receptionist was also adept at elusiveness. After much Bulgarian gesticulating by Blago, a tired impassioned attendant finally shuffled to her place. She confiscated our passports as is common in Eastern Europe and dictated our tariff in dollars, a price which we would later discover to be both inaccurate and inflated enormously beyond that for a Bulgarian, but just right, so they rationalized, for a 'rich' American.

Sleep came soon in our spartan room despite the soft mattress that bowed to the floor and the blaring television from the lobby below.

We arose early the next morning. The time change from Houston was still playing the usual games on our diurnal rhythm. We were greeted in the lobby by Blago, somewhat surprised to see us up and about. Fortunately, someone had turned off the television and the doorman had not yet arrived to take up his post on the couch.

"Let me show you to the dining hall." Blago began. "Once you have taken your breakfast, we will talk of our plans."

At the dining hall doorway, a tall male attendant carefully crossed our names off the list as we handed him our breakfast coupons. In the days to come, we would discover lists to be everywhere and apparently a necessity of life in Bulgaria. As we passed through the door, we entered a cavernous room with long dark curtains on all sides. Round tables of various shapes were draped with faded tablecloths which were littered with crumbs from previous diners.

Breakfast buffet consisted of lukewarm 'hot plates' with various types of sausage, cheese, and eggs. Teabags were available, but not hot water. Stale bread and chalky butter were, however, in great abundance. Both of us began to covet our granola bars secured in our bags upstairs.

I began to notice the attendant who had earlier marked off our names. His deep set eyes were almost constantly focused in our direction. I began to wonder about his past. I then contemplated whether his past would have anything to do with our future.

"We are wholeheartedly behind your efforts. It will be a blessing to all Bulgarians and to us in particular. But you must be extremely careful!" Blago responded once we divulged our plan. "You are not in America. The authorities may now call themselves socialists, but they are the same communist who confiscated church property, burned Bibles and imprisoned hundreds of Christians for over forty years."

The stench of the cigarettes of the night before still hung heavily in the air. The small group sitting in the overstuffed black lobby chairs was quiet with unspoken agreement with Blago's sentiments. Their obvious concern with retribution was not baseless. The ruthlessness of the Darzhavna Sigurnost (State Security Police) was well known, even in the west. After all, the Sigurnost was allegedly behind the attempted assassination of Pope John Paul II in St. Peter's Square on May 13, 1981. Each of these pastors sitting around us had borne deprivation and had been terrorized for their Faith. All could personally demonstrate the scars communism had wrought.

"Let us assure you. We will be wise. We will follow the Holy Ghost. We are presenting this humanitarian medical aid plan to the Minister of Health this afternoon." Sue responded.

I quickly concurred. These Bulgarians, I thought, were very wary about new ideas. I also considered, however, that I had never lived under the shadow of the Sigurnost.

Nicolai ushered us out front. On the street we approached a small red Lada, the Russian-made 'car of the people'. All I had heard about its unreliability would soon be demonstrated.

"This is our 'special car'." Nicolai began in his broken English. "My cousin owns it. He asked me to bring it back to Varna when he heard of my trip here to Sofia."

"Please get in." He invited. "We will escort you to your appointment at the Ministry of Health.

As we deposited ourselves onto the cold upholstery, he continued. "This is Alexi."

Alexi turned from his position in the front passenger seat. He wore a black beard and a blue sock hat. His breath turned white as he greeted us with a toothy smile.

Nicolai struggled into the driver's seat. With a lurch and a grind, he shifted into gear and we were off. I turned to see the Moscow Park Hotel in daylight for the first time. It was, as I expected, classic Eastern European design with faded blue windows affixed to unpainted concrete. A gaudy iron fountain out front stood rusting and waterless. In the distance, impersonal apartment houses of similar drab design reached into the overcast sky. Leafless black locust, poplar, and chestnut trees lined the wide avenue leading to the city center. As we descended a gentle hill, a grimy electric tram filled with faceless people struggled up the street in the opposite direction. Its metal wheels constantly screeching against the track.

It was our turn to struggle as we began to ascend another gentle grade. Nicolai gestured towards the occasional Mercedes and Ford Escorts among the old trucks and worn-out taxis. "The communists, as you can see, have turned into the best capitalists."

Once in Sofia proper, Nicolai turned into an alley lined with small shops. He carefully maneuvered the car onto the sidewalk and killed the ignition.

"Alexi will stay with the car." He said. "Otherwise, the local mafia will take from it what they want."

I suppose my expression gave away my thoughts, because Nicolai laughed and then said, "Yes, brother, the mafia will steal in broad daylight. And they will steal even a broken down car as this. During tough times, even the mafia is not choosy."

Dr. Ivan Kourtev, the acting Minister of Health, met us in the sparse but crowded lobby. After cordial introductions, he escorted us past the security desk, to a small lift. The narrow doorway necessitated single file entry. He manually closed the doors and pushed a black button. With a jerk and grind the elevator rumbled to the third floor. His office was sparse, lined with bookshelves packed with yellowing magazines and journals, most in the cyrillic script. The very few bound volumes were stacked precariously against the window. A faded map of Bulgaria draped the wall behind his desk. He offered seats on a couch covered with clay-colored vinyl which we accepted.

"What can I do for you?" Without a pause he gestured towards Nicolai and continued. "Pastor Kokonchez has advised me of your interest in helping our country."

As he lit his cigarette, I advised him of our plan to provide medical assistance in a Church-based clinic. "...We will provide medications only if you allow for their free importation and safe delivery to the designated clinic." I was thinking of Alexi sitting in our car on the street below. U.S. made medications, I assumed, would have a higher street value than Russian made car parts.

"Of course, we also would like permission for an occasional medical team from the West to practice within the clinic," I continued.

He took a long drag from his cigarette and slowly leaned forward, both elbows firmly planted amongst the pile of papers and soft-bound journals on his desk. "What makes you think we need your assistance?" Each word was accompanied by exhaled cigarette smoke.

"Because two years ago," I immediately responded, " President Zhelev (the Bulgarian head of state) wrote the pastor of my church in America requesting immediate medical humanitarian aid. His letter was accompanied by a similar plea from your predecessor, Dr. Ivan Kirov, documenting the specific medications in greatest need." As I spoke I presented copies of these letters for his review. After a pause, I continued, "We responded by shipping a large quantity of medications to meet your need."

After a brief delay, his demeanor had changed and he responded with gratitude, "On behalf of my government and the Bulgarian people, I deeply thank you for your benevolence. Today we are not in such dire straights, yet ours is a medical system in development." With a laugh, he continued, "You know, both of our countries are going through a medical system transition; we from possibly the worst medical system, you from the best. Ultimately, it appears that we will meet somewhere in between."

"We, of course, will not refuse any further benevolence on your part and will do everything within our power to facilitate your efforts. But there already is a model for what you propose in the city of Rousse. A functioning evangelical polyclinic has been established by a Bible School there. Perhaps you could talk with them to help you get started."

5 NOV

Dr. Todor Shirov met us on the street just outside Sofia City Hospital Academia

#1. He was thin and slight in stature. Yet his eyes and smile revealed his Christian heart.

After preliminary greetings he turned to lead us into the bowels of the hospital towards his office. We maneuvered around the hoards of people loitering outside and entered through what appeared to be a side entrance. Inside it was dark, damp, and cold. The morning chill still hung heavily in the air which made the bare cement walls and dark tile floors appear even colder. Our breath appearing as white vapor also argued against the presence of any significant heating source within the building.

Soon we exited to enter a courtyard. Bare earth which pools of water had turned to mud was interrupted occasionally by clumps of dead grass and broken benches. We avoided the mud by staying on the uneven, cracked sidewalk which led to the left towards another multistoried building. Icy wind blew down from above causing us all to tighten our coats.

Inside we immediately ascended a dark stairwell to the second floor. Apparently, we had entered a patient ward as many attached to glass bottles of intravenous fluids sat in wooden chairs lining the hall. All wore ragged hospital gowns and forlorn faces.

Dr. Shirov lead on through a set of double doors. We now faced additional curious faces yet all in miniature.

"The pediatric oncology ward," Dr. Shirov explained.

Suddenly our hearts were pierced with the hopelessness that abounded here. In my years of training and medical practice, I had never gotten used to children with cancer. When I think of how the devil could afflict the innocent, I am reminded of his depravity and barbarism. But especially among these little boys and girls was his presence evident. We saw no toys in their extremely spartan rooms; only several miniature cots with rusting frames and brownish-yellow sheets. One filthy window in each room begrudgingly allowed rays of sunlight to enter. A small radiator of questionable usefulness fixed itself to one wall. Beige paint flaked from all walls and cobwebs were at every corner.

We saw not one thin boy grinning nor one gaunt girl smiling.

Down the hall, we passed a wheelchair whose design had to be of the early 1900's. Three of its four corners had a small wheel. The fourth had none. Nevertheless it was occupied by an emaciated and listless child.

Dr. Shirov led on to the operating suite. He paused to greatly emphasize that we were not allowed inside in our street clothes. We acknowledged our understanding as such was common to normal infection control procedure. He then led us around to a side hallway and paused, motioning towards a screen window. His proud countenance associated with this small window at first made little sense. We soon realized his intent was for us to look at the room behind the screen. Simultaneously we stepped to our left and bent forward. Our gaze revealed an old woman spreading a bucket full of gray water across an operating room floor with a dirty mop. My eyes then focused on the screen. It was rusty and broken. A fly buzzed through a small hole on the right side. Sue looked at me and I at her. We immediately read each other's thoughts.

The pharmacy was next. Dr. Shirov and the pharmacy director took obvious pride in the brochures hanging on the otherwise bare walls. Many advertized antibiotics common to my practice in the U.S.A.

"So you have unasyn and claforan?" I asked.

They both paused and looked at each other as if waiting for the other to answer first. Finally, the pharmacy director slowly responded in broken English, "We no have medicines in pictures." She was referring to the brochures with her hands as she spoke. "Government has limited monthly budget for medicines. When monthly budget gone, no more medicines."

"But what about infections?" Sue asked. "You do have some basic antibiotics?"

"Oh, yes, we do have. But only at Infectious Disease Hospital."

"But what about prophylactic antibiotics for surgery here in this hospital?" I asked.

"We do not use. Antibiotics too expensive. Use restricted to Infectious Disease Hospital."

"What about the chemotherapy for the children we just saw?" Sue asked.

Dr. Shirov answered, "When the budget for the month runs out, we don't have the chemotherapy to mix and administer. Usually, by the tenth of each month, the budget has been exhausted."

After a pause, he added, "Yes, Dr. and Mrs. Price, we are not well supplied. We Bulgarians have learned to do without."

BULGARIA — NOVEMBER 1993

6 NOV

"Be downstairs no later than 8:30 A.M," we had remembered Blago state the previous evening. Therefore, when we were downstairs at the appointed time, we wondered why Blago was so surprised.

"O.K. We have a slight change in plans. Check out of the hotel and have your bags packed and downstairs no later than 10:30."

At 10:30 we were checked out and waiting in the overstuffed chairs that wreaked of tobacco. We were still there at 11:00. At 11:30 Sue asked me whether we were in the right place. I reassured her that we were. By 12:00 I had checked several meeting rooms on the first three floors for a familiar face. None was found. 12:30 found me contemplating which airline had two available seats out of Bulgaria that afternoon.

Blago and Nicolai appeared at 12:45. Between their profuse apologies, we ultimately realized that an important meeting had delayed their arrival. Our bags were deposited in the back seat of Nicolai's 'special car', the red lada. We also deposited ourselves on these cold vinyl back seats. Grinding gears and a sticky clutch bolted us backwards as we lurched towards the highway leading to the Black Sea.

An hour later we were well into the Balkan Mountains when Nicolai, with his wife, Elly, at his side, turned into a rest stop beside the highway. Blago and his wife, who were following behind us in his small Toyota, also pulled to a stop. We soon enjoyed sandwiches of cheese and salami on the parking lot beneath golden and orange leaves of poplar, beech, chestnut, and black locust. Green pines and furs surrounded a spring that trickled water off brown rocks. The noise of an occasional passing vehicle only added to the serenity of God's creation. I contemplated to myself that even in a country defiled by atheistic shortsightedness, God's fingerprint was evident.

We were soon back on the road, yet Sue and I had switched to Blago's Toyota. As the miles rolled by, Blago began to explain the spiritual situation within Bulgaria.

"In 1989, when the communist government fell, Nicolai and I held many evangelistic meetings across the country. Millions were exposed for the first time to the gospel of Jesus Christ," Blago explained. "We even held a great rally in the very town square of the village we just passed through."

I recalled the agricultural village of brick and stone in the midst of harvested wheat fields. We had maneuvered around groups of goats and sheep in the middle of the street. Shepherd boys hurriedly herded them off the thorough-fare with sticks as we approached.

"Thousands received Jesus as their personal savior. Many local Churches were borne out of these efforts; not just ours, but those of Christian workers across the land. Our denomination alone went from thirty to three hundred local Churches!"

He paused to allow us to digest this information. "We Bulgarians have a long history of Christianity. We are the Macedonia that Paul evangelized in the first century. We also were the people who prevented the Ottoman Turks from spreading their Moslem faith across Europe." As he spoke, I recalled how Bulgaria had been ruled by the Moslem Ottoman Empire for over seven hundred years during which time they had been treated as slaves in their own land. Atrocities of every kind had been forced upon them. (The current crisis in neighboring Balkan countries at least partly stems from such memories.) An active armed resistance, erratic as it was, was sufficient to embroil the ruling Ottomans. It was true that had it not been for Bulgaria, the rest of Europe may well have had a koran-based society.

"But now our freedom to preach the Gospel is under attack. No longer are we allowed to preach freely and openly in public places. Some of the larger Churches, such as Nicolai's in Varna, who are forced to rent public buildings for their Sunday services, are finding rental fees way beyond their means."

"Why must they rent public buildings?" I asked.

"Because so many received Jesus that existing Church buildings are too small to hold them all." After a pause, he continued, "That in itself, would not be such a bad problem, if it were not for the forces within the Orthodox Church and the news media."

"What do you mean?" I asked.

"I mean that the government of the 'enlightened socialists' has labeled evangelicals as sects. We therefore are not allowed to utilize radio nor televi-sion to spread the Gospel. The news media and established Church has seem-ingly cooperated to denounce us at every opportunity."

Fields of cut wheat surrounded our lonely car on highway 6 as we approached Kazanlak. A gray sky overhead seemed to add a certain dreariness to Blago's words.

But he soon added, "Our interest in a church-based medical clinic as you propose could conceivably help us in many ways. You could help us gain respectability among the people and at the same time add another way to make

Jesus known for who He is!"

Kilometers later with dusk upon us and darkness rapidly approaching, we switched back into the red lada. Blago and his wife were to go no farther. They would stay in this village not far from his own Church in Jambol. We would travel on in the night, across the final hump of the Balkans to the Black Sea coastal city of Varna.

Night fell quickly as we pulled away from Blago's village. "I will need to stop for another quart of oil!" Nicolai yelled over the clamoring engine of the laboring lada.

At the next crossroads, Nicolai turned into a dimly lit gas station. Trucks laden with goods from Hungary were parked haphazardly to the side as their respective drivers loitered nearby. Just beyond Nicolai's hunched back I could see the small engine dwarfed by empty space under the hood.

Soon, we had penetrated the mountain slopes. As the headlights flickered off and on, mostly off, I was glad when a car suddenly appeared from nowhere behind us. It's bright lights, I had reasoned, would help Nicolai gauge the road ahead. However, Nicolai appeared even the more distressed. Suddenly, we approached another gas station. Abruptly, Nicolai pulled in. The car behind us also sharply braked to enter behind us. As I withdrew from the backseat, I could see four men begin to slowly exit the mercedes behind us. But hastily, they sat back down in their seats as if they had simultaneously changed their minds. Not a word was spoken amongst them. Nicolai, meanwhile, was fumbling with the gas nozzle as he nervously glanced back towards the mercedes. He had not turned off his engine and its idle began to produce abundant choking smoke. Much too soon, he was finished and curtly told me to get back into the car as he shuffled 100 leva to the attendant. Strange behavior, I had thought. I also wondered, if we had needed gas so urgently, why had we not gotten it when we filled the crankcase with oil just a few minutes previously? Days later I discovered the reason behind this strange turn of events which made me ever so thankful for God's protecting angels. Nicolai was concerned and nervous because these were Mafia controlled mountain roads. Those who traveled in nice cars, like mercedes, worked for the Mafia. All others rode in cars like ours. That night we were the prey and the hunted. Obviously, however, the angels of the Lord had surrounded us and protected us!

Quickly, we were on the road again. The mercedes had not followed which made for an extremely dark night when the lights went out for good in the tunnel. Outside the tunnel, we weaved from one side of the road to the other. At first, Nicolai had his head behind the windshield. Soon, his upper body was contorted outside the window in his vain attempts to see better.

A few hundred feet of this felt like miles.

"We will go to the next village." Nicolai had braked the car to a complete stop and turned to face us in the backseat. "I know the Pastor of the small Church. She will help us." He slowly accelerated and let the dim lights of the mountain village ahead be our guide. A few turns later, we pulled to a stop beside a dark cement block dwelling.

The family, consisting of the grandmother, grandfather and two children, were asleep but quickly arose to welcome us. Nicolai rushed over to the local pastor's house to phone his cousin in Varna. "He will come to pick us up." Nicolai had assured us. "After all, it was his broken down lada that got us into this mess."

Inside the simple brick house, flies were thick and pesty. The table was covered with a greasy oil cloth, the windows with tattered curtains, and the walls with a faded coat of paint. The children had been sleeping in a cot in the middle of the only room which we maneuvered around to sit at straight back wooden chairs at the table. Burlap sacks of wormy apples and small potatoes leaned against one wall. The only evidence of convenience was a black-and-white TV.

Outside, the garden had been recently tilled. A grape arbor over the garden provided little shelter from the cool wind. In the distance, a screeching train penetrated the night air.

Nicolai returned and showed us the little church building constructed by the grandfather on his precious land by his own hands. He had accepted Jesus early in his adult life, we were told. He stood smiling and nodding his approval of Nicolai's narration. (He apparently knew a little English, but not enough to speak it, or so we gathered.) His wife was also a believer for many years. Because of their stand for Jesus, their staunchly Orthodox families and others had driven them from the village of their birth. Then his wife was stricken with stomach cancer. Way up in this mountain village, far from any medical help, they desperately prayed to their God. Jesus answered by healing her to the amazement of everyone! They then decided to build this small church as a testimony for Jesus in their adopted village. Now, approximately 40 attend services there. 'Grandfather' shot proud glances our way as we took our turn in smiling and nodding approval.

We returned to the house and found the grandmother frying eggs on an outside grill. She insisted upon preparing us a meal despite our objections and the late hour; all the time chattering away in a rapid fire of Bulgarian with Nicolai and Lilly.

At the table we found our plates with eggs floating in a pool of grease accompanied by cabbage salad and brewed root tea. (I guess it just wouldn't be Bulgarian without the grease.) The bread rested on the same oily tablecloth that seconds ago harbored scores of flies. I recalled the outhouse, just a few feet outside the open window, smelling of sewage. The flies had obviously been there as well. Our appetites weren't too keen yet we ate what was set before us.

As Nicolai and Lilly sopped up the last of the grease (we politely left ours congealing on our plates), Nicolai's cousin arrived in a beat-up miniature station wagon. The bags and medical supplies were transferred and we were on our way. Twelve hours and 470 kilometers after we had departed Sofia, we arrived safely in Varna.

7 NOV

The 600 to 700 Bulgarians that made up the Pentecostal Church, Varna, which Nicolai pastors, greeted us warmly at the theater. I declared the healing power of the risen Christ and the Holy Ghost did a work. Because the theater was rented, the service lasted only two hours. Yet many came forward for prayer and followed Sue and I as we headed to our car. They were so hungry for God!

That evening, the Church celebrated the reopening of their small church building that the communist government of Bulgaria had seized 30 years previously. The communists had used it as a warehouse for books authored by Marx, Lenin and Engels. During the recent democracy movement, the people of Varna burned the books.

Nicolai had reported that when the books were burned, he suddenly had a burden to pray for repossession. He then traveled to Houston to attend meetings at Lakewood Church. While there, Pastor Osteen called him out and prophesied that he would 'repossess the land'. A few months later, out of the blue, the new government contacted him, wondering if he was interested in having the building back free of charge!

Now, instead of works by Marx, Engels, and Lenin, there are works authored by God. God's works are the people serving Him here. The building is small; definitely not room enough for the 700 members. Yet it is centrally located in the center of town and Nicolai plans to use its courtyard for a bigger and expanded auditorium.

8 NOV

Sue and I distributed a portion of the medical supplies to the medical personnel. Afterwards, four physicians, a medical student, and several nurses lingered to hear my testimony of healing. Night had already fallen and we were again in the repossessed church. I simply shared how I repossessed my health with the Word of God!

I then offered to assist them in setting up a clinic, or as the Bulgarian Minister of Health had defined it, a polyclinic, here in their own Church. Nicolai had already spoken of including a clinic as part of the building program he had envisioned for the courtyard. For those who were raised in a system where the paycheck came from the government, a private enterprise such as what we proposed remained quite foreign to them. Needless to say, they had many questions. But I reminded them of a similar enterprise functioning within Bulgaria at a Bible school in Rousse. They decided to send a representative up to this school on the Danube and see what was required. From the looks of things, the main requirement they already possessed; faith. They just hadn't realized it yet.

9 NOV

The turboprop's engines roared through the November sky. We had decided to return to Sofia high over the Balkans rather than on them. An hour flight was much preferred to another fourteen hours on the road.

Our flight had been delayed by two hours as we waited for the ground fog to lift. During the delay, I wandered through Varna's small airport departure lounge. Few people were there, just some discarded brochures about Moscow and Kiev. The faded colors on these somehow did not correlate well with their exuberant descriptions. My knowledge of the total breakdown of the public health system of the former U.S.S.R. made such destinations unappealing.

Yet I knew God had not forsaken Moscow nor Kiev. He would make a way for them, just as He was making a way for Bulgaria.

He had made a way for Nicolai to repossess his church. He had made a way for Blago to maintain his evangelical desire. We had crossed the Mafia-infested Balkans in the night without headlights with a load of expensive medical supplies: He obviously made a way for us.

Down below were the rocky Balkan slopes. I remembered the witness of the grandmother and grandfather. God had not left them defenseless either and made a way for them. There were many others down there, represented by woodsmoke, villages and farms. God remembers them, too.

The engine droned on. Maybe we will return someday to set up clinics on these very slopes. Maybe we will help supply Bulgarian doctors and nurses with medications and supplies to do so.

Once in Sofia, I would try to arrange for an earlier flight back home. Sue and I both missed our two small boys. We longed to hug them again.

God also misses His children. He longs to draw near to His little Bulgarian boys and girls.

We were now above the clouds and way above the fog. Overhead, the Bulgarian sun was shining brightly.

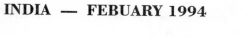

New Delhi •

INDIA FEBUARY 1994

Calcutta•

• Bombay

Trivandrum •

2 FEB

"Sthothram, sthothram, sthothram! Karthavai sthothram!"

I could hear the Malayalam voices in the foyer. Many poor had come to the free medical clinics sponsored by the local Church. The pastor and those assisting him had spontaneously broken out in praises to our Lord Jesus. They were busily registering the sick, yet despite the press of warm feverish bodies closely around them on a hot humid day, their joy was demonstrated by their praises.

"Giddiness, sir."

I was in the room off to the side of the foyer surveying the crowd through the bars on the window. Mary, the retired Indian nurse who had come all the way from Alleppey via bus was directing me to my next patient.

77

"Giddiness, sir, and overall weakness."

I turned from the window to face a frail, young, sari-clad mother and her two children. The boy, in shorts and a faded t-shirt was ten; his sister, three. Despite their obvious poverty and purulent nasal drainage, they both wore huge smiles. Both had bronchitis and sinusitis and required ampicillin. The mother, by complaining of giddiness, was indicating that she wanted vitamins. Indeed, her conjunctivae were pale, evidence of anemia.

"Give her the prenatal ones."

She wasn't pregnant but the prenatal vitamins had a high iron percentage which her diet was not providing. I wondered how often and what she ate, considering her thin frame.

"Oh, and give the children the smaller vitamins."

I was hoping a short supply of vitamins would at least replenish their meager diets for the time being and thereby assist them in fighting off their present infections. I knew the commonest cause of immune deficiency worldwide is malnutrition. Such was being fully represented in the clinic so far today. My two and a half year old back home was a giant compared to this little girl.

Mary directed them to the pharmacist. Of course, he was not really a pharmacist but he had once worked in a Kerala hospital, he could count and, when he heard of my coming, had boned-up on the latin abbreviations used commonly in prescriptions. When I arrived that morning, Alexander advised me that he would be our pharmacist.

"Do you know QID?" I questioned.

"Four times a day, sir!", he quickly shouted.

"And BID?"

"Twice a day, sir!"

He was treating me as if I was his military drill sergeant. His eagerness to please and work was obvious. He was recruited. I was to learn later of how he was prevented from committing suicide with a lethal combination of drugs by the audible voice of God. His eagerness to help me was a demonstration of his love of the God who saved him.

As the mother was ushered to the next room, she abruptly turned, bowed her head slightly with her hands together, fingers pointing upward just beneath her chin and smiled; the Asian demonstration of gratitude and respect. There were tears in her eyes. I wondered if she or her children had ever seen a doctor before.

By the end of the day, I had seen 39 patients. I had been expecting more. Yet a very good turnout considering the local Trivandrum government would not allow public advertising of these free clinics. Nevertheless, 6 of the 39 gave their hearts to Jesus: six new citizens of heaven; six more to antagonize the devil!

3 FEB

"Primary complex, sir."

Mary again was across the table from me, the little boy and his mother were at her side. Malayalam to me was a jumble of uninterpretable sounds and tones; more like gibberish than a language. My untrained ear could not distinguish when one word ended and another began. I often found myself wondering if they were all faking it and putting me on. But after bantering back and forth for several minutes, the child's mother and Mary had obviously communicated. Mary had turned to me to repeat his diagnosis given to him by the doctors at the medical college only a year before. His mother handed me the faded and worn card with both hands, as is the Asian custom. I scanned his medical history and diagnosis written in English, and turned to the boy. He was nine, but my guess would have put him no older than five. I suppose his little body was doing its best to fight off the bacteria that had raged in his lungs and other organs. He probably had other problems as well, such as intestinal worms. His stomach was bloated and his oral mucosa pale, circumstantial evidence of such. He had been treated for the bacteria but had recently begun to cough once again. His concerned mother heard from her neighbors about the free clinic and therefore brought her little boy to see the American doctor. I turned again to the mother. Her eyes were full of fear.

"Any blood?", I asked.

Again this prompted an exchange of uninterpretable sounds.

"No blood only purulent yellow sputum and high fever."

I auscultated his lungs and found coarse breath sounds at the apices, high up in his chest, anteriorly. With each breath I could see his intercostal muscles straining between his very prominent ribs. In the days of the British Raj they called the effects of this bacteria consumption. Today we call it tuberculosis.

"Give him some amoxicillin for his purulent cough and some vitamins for malnutrition. But stress that she must take him back to the medical college for a comparison X-ray as soon as possible. I am concerned that he may have a relapse and will need additional therapy."

He was the 34th patient of the day. I would see another 21 before the day was done. They complained of wheezing, loose movements (diarrhea), intestinal worms, scabies, generalized itch, skin ulcers and boils, nonspecific joint and back pain, cough (productive and nonproductive), and the ever present 'giddiness'. We had medicines for them all. Most, due to multiple illnesses, received more than one type of medication. All also accepted prayer. Nineteen received Jesus that day to bring the two-day total to twenty-five.

My next patient, a young woman, was complaining of kidney problems.

"She already has kidney surgery scheduled." Mary said.

"Tell her there is not much I can do except provide pain medicines and vitamins."

As an afterthought, I added, "...and we can pray."

I would later discover how important that afterthought would be.

4 FEB

Alexander had begun to invite all the patients to return for the nightly worship meetings. He had been working furiously each day, assisting the pharmacist and the local believers. He was ensuring that all received prayer and spiritual counseling about the one true Creator God. He had a group of pastors counseling and praying on a one-to-one basis scattered throughout the building.

"Why are you asking them to come to the meetings?, I asked.

"Because I know how Indians think. They place great significance on a person of authority - in this instance, you - laying hands on them individually and praying. Or, as they see it, conveying a blessing."

So they came. They brought their friends, neighbors and other family members. And they also came to Jesus. Sixty-seven were seen by me in the clinic that day. Forty-five of these hindus turned to Christ.

"Sthothram, sthothram, sthothram. Karthavai sthothram! Dievathinu sthothram!"

The pastors were praising God for the harvest. As they prayed and counseled each patient, their excitement was growing. The fields truly were white ready for reaping. The medical work was like a great scythe in gathering souls for the kingdom of God.

The first night I had spoken about divine healing, referring to Revelation 3:8 and including my personal testimony of healing. The following night my topic was overcoming fear. Tonight I would see great demonstrations of Holy Ghost power!

"Then Jesus said to the twelve, 'Do you also want to go away?' Then Simon Peter answered Him, 'Lord, to whom shall we go? You have the words of eternal life.'"

As I waited for Alexander to interpret the passage from John 6 that I had just quoted, I considered my audience. This service was truly Indian. All were seated on mats, the women on my right, the men on my left. Their praises to God consisted of clapping and singing with an intensity that only severe per-secution could foster. All shoes were left in the foyer. No female's head was left uncovered.

Each night, the crowd had grown. Tonight, the mats were packed. Alexander was correct, the people were interested in receiving a blessing.

The church building itself was very nice. Yet the vaulted ceilings, stained glass windows, panelled walls and plush carpet common to churches in America were absent. The beauty of this simple Indian Church was not the furnishings nor the decor, it was in the people, former heathen, praising our God.

Alexander was finished and awaiting my next phrase.

"By following Jesus we have direction, deliverance and dominion: direction because we can be assured of going to heaven; deliverance from the devil and demon powers; and dominion because Jesus has Given us the right to be called sons and daughters of the most high God - the Living God!"

The Holy Ghost was present. He was directing the meeting. Many were saved. The exact number is unknown due to the rush. Many were set free. Six testified of the miraculous. One of the six was a woman I recognized. I saw her in the clinic the day before. She was the one scheduled for kidney surgery.

Alexander held the microphone for her as she began to speak. Abraham posi-tioned himself close to my ear and interpreted her words.

"I had been under the care of doctors at the medical college", she began. "I had been told that I needed kidney surgery and the date had been set. But someone told me about the free medical clinic and the American doctor so I thought I would give him a chance. So I came and saw the doctor. Yet when he prayed, I felt something."

Tears began to well up in her eyes and her voice broke.

"I felt the presence of God!"

Everybody began to praise God. The Malayalam voices no longer sounded strange, but seemed as natural as my own native tongue. I could distinguish the deep baritone voice of the pastor resonating above the rest, "Sthothrum, sthothrum, sthrotrum! Praise the Lord, praise the Lord, praise the Lord!"

She regained her composure and readjusted her sari.

"So I went back to the doctor at the medical college. He re-examined me and then cancelled my surgery. I am healed!"

Again everyone began to praise Jesus and a rush of Indians crowded the front, both men and women. Others testified of instant deliverance from pain. One reported resolution of 'cloudy vision'. Another claimed freedom from alcohol. The PA system recorded every word. As usual, some PA speakers were strategically placed on the roof to broadcast these proceedings out into the heathen night. No doubt, we will meet some in Heaven because of these witnesses that even the church walls could not contain.

5 FEB

Crowds of men, women, boys and girls were awaiting me when I arrived at the clinic. I suppose the word had gotten out.

About mid-morning I was examining an old man with obvious aching joints by the deliberate way he made every move. I recalled how painful my hip had once been; how I moved very carefully as to not aggravate the pain that no medication could control. But then Jesus touched me and now I am free from pain! My heart went out to this grandfather. He was wearing the typical south Indian dhoti (skirt) and a stained shirt. He had gray stubble on his chin and very few teeth in the midst of swollen gums. He had produced a small bottle with a rusty lid filled with stones.

Mary explained, "He just wanted you to see the stones they removed from his left kidney many years ago."

At that he lifted up his shirt to reveal a nephrectomy scar surrounded by leathery skin.

"He really wants you to pray because his children have left him and he is alone." Mary continued, "You understand that without children he has no hope of surviving. There is no social welfare system here in Kerala. No children, no food. He is very depressed, sir."

" Give him some vitamins. Reassure him that we will pray and will expect Jesus to help him. Remind him of the meeting tonight."

As he shuffled out the door, Alexander came in.

"Praise the Lord, brother!" He was exuberant. Praise the Lord! Those from all castes are coming!"

"Amen!" I responded.

"But you do not understand the significance! Under normal circumstances, the higher castes would never come to a Christian Church. Yet they are coming for the medicines and when we pray, they also accept Jesus!"

"Are you sure?" I asked. "We need to be sure we are not exaggerating."

"Brother, when we see the tears in their eyes, we can be sure."

His gentle rebuke was well taken.

Later that day, an elderly Hindu lady came complaining of back pain and cough. I prescribed ibuprofen and sulfa. She turned somewhat in her seat to reveal a strange tattoo on her right arm.

"What's that?" I asked Mary.

"That's her god. She also has these charms." Mary was indicating a necklace with a series of safety pins attached. "She has told me that when she was a little girl, her parents had the tattoo placed.

"Tell her that Jesus healed me of the same kind of pain with which she is suffering. Also ask her what her god has done for her."

Mary spoke in Malayalam. As she did, the woman turned to me. I needed no interpretation. Her downcast eyes and nervous grin indicated recognition of the One True God.

7 FEB

The Indian-made Ambassador automobile was hurtling through the traffic. Abraham was at the wheel, weaving between a multitude of motorized rickshaws, antiquated cars, and over-laden trucks. Every now and then, the thick diesel smoke from a passing bus forced its way through the open windows.

I was in the back seat contemplating how good an air conditioner would be. Alexander was busy gibbering instructions to Abraham in Malayalam. Long ago I had learned not to watch the road too carefully while in Asian traffic. I had resigned myself to 'ride by faith, not by sight'. Yet many times I found myself watching too closely when there was a sudden increase in the decibel level of the constant horn honking.

Finally, we arrived at the Trivandrum Airport. I don't know why we were surprised to discover that my flight to Bombay was delayed. We sat down in three fiberglass chairs just off the tarmac inside the terminal. The whirling fans overhead kept us comfortable despite the heat and humidity.

I pulled out the map of Kerala I had purchased at the airport newsstand. Alexander showed me the Malabar area of northern Kerala and then Gudalir in the neighboring state of Tamil Nadu.

"...many Moslems here," he was saying as he pointed to these areas on the map.

"Where are the waterways you were talking about?" I asked referring to his desire to provide medical care to a very under-served area. His finger went down the coast of the Arabian Sea, south of Cochin to Alleppey and Kottayan districts.

"And don't forget about the coastal areas south of Trivandrum."

He was referring to the villages we had passed through. I recalled the women squatting the Asian way over piles of stones, pounding them incessantly with crude hammers, making pebbles for roadways and for cement. I remembered also other villages where coconut husk was being woven into rope. A quaint picturesque view from a distance, yet up close the smells of raw sewage and animal waste permeated every breath. The hoards of flies always reminded my medical mind to keep my mouth shut. The dirt floors would serve as breeding grounds for legions of hookworm that would steal the hard-fought-for nutrition from the young and the old. And then there were the many laborers I had seen pulling overloaded carts of banana stalks, coconuts, and burlap sacks of cement. Their already tired muscles would strain even more when a passing bus or truck would hurtle down the road, honking much and missing them by little. For such they would receive 70 rupees per day, about $2.33. I recalled those I had seen in the clinics with worms, tuberculosis, typhoid fever, malaria, and even simple body aches. I remembered those in despair due to loss of a husband leaving them widowed with several small children to feed in a land with little social consciousness. All of these cannot even dream of what most Americans take for granted as basic necessities because they do not know that such luxury exists.

As Abraham and Alexander rose to go back to the car, Abraham turned to me, grabbed both my arms and began to pray. "I pray that your medical practice is blessed, your wife is blessed and your children are blessed. That God will keep you and protect you."

I bowed my head in the middle of the airport in that heathen land.

"I pray that this is only the beginning for you," he continued. "That the Holy Ghost will bring you and your wife back to us here in Kerala and that a mighty medical ministry will be established among the heathen. And thereby Kerala will never be the same!"

In my few days in Kerala, I had dispensed 9740 tablets and pills in treating 317 patients. 119 of the 317 had received Jesus. Others were saved, set free from bondage and miraculously healed by the power of the Holy Ghost in the 6 meetings in which I spoke.

"Sthothram, karthavai sthothram!" I said. "Praise the Lord!"

I could see the land as the plane rose to the clouds. Jesus had taught of how the good shepherd would leave the ninety-nine sheep for just one that was lost. He Himself had left the comforts of heaven for each one of us. I am praying that laborers for this harvest will leave the comforts of their lives for His purpose. I am sure the Holy Ghost will have His way in this land and indeed, Kerala will never be the same.

Manila ·

PHILIPPINES JUNE 1994

· Cebu
· Tagbilaran
Dumaquete· · Apo

2 JUNE

"How long has she been like this?" I asked.

"Since her last child was born; several months."

I had heard a similar response before, while in Nepal. That poor Nepali woman died shortly thereafter. This woman also appeared near death. She lay listlessly on her mat, cachectic and emaciated. Her joints protruded from surrounding atrophied muscle and exhausted subcutaneous tissue. She was much too weak to even lift her head to greet me, yet with a slow deliberate blink of her eyelids, she acknowledged my presence.

I returned slowly to my seat near the front of the now crowded little church. Songs of praise to our God filled the room as well as the surrounding barrio through the open doors and screen-less windows. Rotating fans did little to ward off the sweltering humid heat of the Manila night.

I rejoined my wife, Sue, on the first row. I was exhausted from our recent flight. Perspiration glued my clothes to my back; the same clothes that I had now been wearing for the past 72 hours. We had arrived very late the previous evening aboard Northwest flight 001, but our bags with fresh clothing had remained in Tokyo. After the service we would battle the jeepneys once again to Ninoy Aquino International Airport to collect our luggage. Of course, the flight would be late and our bags last off the carousel.

Presently, however, I excused myself to lean against a nearby wall. The praise and worship was wonderful but I was falling asleep where I stood. I needed some support before I fell flat on my face. As I leaned, I turned once again to glance at the girl on her palate. She appeared to be hopeless. Yet something inside me told me differently.

Pastor Merciano Driz turned to me. "The service will be yours once we complete praise and worship. Many have come from other churches in our group. We are all excited about this, our first healing service."

Surely, I thought, he was not expecting the invalid girl to walk! But I was also praying that the Holy Ghost would move. I didn't much feel like moving, myself. I fumbled through my New Testament to review my hastily prepared notes of a few hours earlier.

"Rely on Me, not your notes, and I will heal her." It was that 'something' inside me once again.

The praise and worship stopped. Pastor Driz asked Norma to introduce me. Momentarily, I was on the platform testifying of God's ever present healing power.

"...those who desire a divine touch, please come forward..." As I closed with these words, Sue and Norma came up to pray for the many who responded to my invitation. As the crowds came, I noticed the girl still on her bed. She had not moved. I nudged my way through the throng to where she lay.

As I came close, I saw the tears running down both cheeks. Her listlessness and weakness remained. Her tears were those of despair. Those swarming around her also had tears; obviously her family and close friends.

I laid my hands upon her and prayed for strength.

Nothing apparently happened.

I returned to those at the front of the church. Sue was praying with authority as she commanded sicknesses to leave. Norma too was exercising her authority on behalf of those around her. The worship team began anew with songs of praise.

"She felt something!"

I turned to see a man who had been at the girl's side earlier. "She felt something like electricity when you prayed!"

I returned to the girl who still lay motionless on the floor.

"Tell her to do something she was not able to do previously!" I shouted above the surrounding din. But everyone just looked at me and at each other.

"Tell her to get up!" I repeated. The response was the same.

Therefore, I took her by the hand. Momentarily, she stood unassisted and then walked! The tears in her eyes were no longer those of despair, but of joy!

While she walked about with hands upraised to God, Pastor Driz brought my attention to another invalid. A thin old man was propped up in a chair towards the front of the church. His wife and presumably daughter were restraining him from falling to the floor; he didn't even have the strength to sit unassisted in a chair. On the floor lay his foley bag full of urine. He had evidently suffered a stroke and could perform absolutely no basic bodily functions; from his loved ones he was dependent upon total care. Fortunately, these loved ones believed in a miracle working God.

I laid my hands on him and prayed, "...in Jesus name, be healed!"

He started to move his right hand. His wife turned to me and said, "Oh sir! I believe this is only the beginning! I am believing for a complete miracle!"

I looked into her eyes, so filled with hope and faith. I then looked at the man. I knew medically there was no hope. I put my hands on his wife's shoulder, giving her some encouragement. However, my mind told me there was no way.

I would later learn how wrong my mind was.

3 JUNE

Tagolog and other dialects interspersed with filipino English were being mumbled, spoken and shouted. Crowds of filipinos sparred each other for the most opportune position in the nonexistent line. Several roosters within rattan crates crowed. Seven years had lapsed since I had last been here at Manila's Domestic Airport. Little had changed.

Agnes and Norma ushered me through various checkpoints until finally we reached the departure lounge where the chaos was slightly more controlled. There I was reunited with my family. My two blonde haired boys were drawing a crowd of dark-haired filipino children and their parents. Sue appeared rested despite little sleep. To myself I contemplated that few doctor's wives of any nationality would endure the tribulations associated with taking a three and six year old halfway around the world to a foreign culture.

Our flight was abruptly trumpeted via the shrill PA system. A short walk across the scalding tarmac brought us to the stuffy cabin packed with warm bodies with little leg room. Once airborne, the ventilation improved.

Our flight plan took us over Taal Volcano of southern Luzon and then on to Mindoro and Panay. We then crossed Cebu to approach Dumaguete from the south over the Mindanao Sea. The airstrip by the sea received us not so gingerly, the pilot braking hard immediately upon touchdown.

Porters converged on disgorged passengers and their luggage, while pedicab drivers accosted potential customers only after an invisible line was traversed. The crowd behind this line was like a huge amoeba, engulfing passenger and bags together and then spitting them out into the street.

Fortunately for us, we recognized Roberto with Pastor Gordon Apura within the crowd. Pastor Apura had been a professional pharmaceutical sales representative for several years prior to committing himself to the ministry. Initially, he coordinated seminars across the Philippines to provide pastoral training. We soon would benefit from these coordination skills as he provided excellent organization for the medical clinics. He had now been a pastor himself for the past three years. Although he did not yet have a church building, he had involved himself in conducting evangelistic crusades across Negros Oriental, utilizing gospel films. He also had a thriving prison ministry and feeding program for the poor. Recently, he had been invited by public school officials into the classrooms.

"Where would you like to take lunch?" James, our driver was asking. "Perhaps seafood?"

Soon we were in the midst of fresh fish and white rice, the ubiquitous staple of the islands. The restaurant was of nipa construction on stilts. Underneath, a pool of water harbored crabs, and fish (and associated odors), soon to be a customer's lunch or dinner. Andrew and Austin, my two boys, had a great time pointing out this water-life amongst the algae, leaning sometimes precariously over the railing. It is amazing how mud and water draw little boys like magnets.

James soon returned and we were on our way. Our departure had been delayed due to a flat tire, the first of three suffered by the old borrowed van used to transport our medications and medical team. James drove us in the car behind this van for the 50 kilometers to Bais City. Enroute, he pointed out fish ponds, coconut groves, banana trees, salt flats, rice fields and sugar cane plantations whereby most of the populous derived livelihood. The mountains in the background and the sea to our right provided an illusionary idyllic setting. Those in the sweltering fields were covered from head to foot in tattered pieces of cloth, their simplistic protection from the violent ultraviolet rays of the equatorial sun. Fishermen, in their flimsy bancas, plied the treacherous waters just off the coast in the channel between Negros and the island of Cebu, which could be clearly seen in the distance. The sugarcane fields harbored occasional fires, burning chaff and producing black smoke that lazily floated heavenward while workers close by cut cane by machete. This backbreaking labor with minuscule monetary rewards and a multitude of occupational hazards dissolved the illusion of a carefree existence. Life is hard here and disease rampant.

Occasionally, a big truck filled with freshly cut sugarcane barreled our way to force us onto the side of the road. Houston traffic was never like this, at least not in this century. I therefore understood the frequent gasps emanating from June in the back seat.

Just a few kilometers past the smoke belching sugarmill, James turned onto a sidestreet. A few turns later, we arrived at Pastor Bobby's church. Just in front of the church, at the end of the street, a crowd had gathered anticipating the free medical exams that had been advertised to the community. I slowly made my way through the crowd and deposited my bag of instruments on a wooden table near the back of the church.

"Pastor Bobby has an independent work but we cooperate with him frequently", Pastor Apura said as he introduced us. I would learn later how he and his wife had built the church and his home with their own hands. The smiles on their faces hinted of the love their hearts harbored for those around them. Despite tremendous hardships, they had remained true to what God had called them to do in Bais City, without any denominational support.

The church building was simple yet functional. Curtains had been draped to separate rudimentary exam rooms from the pharmacy, triage, registration, and counseling areas. Sue, Roberto, Norma, Agnes and my older son, Andrew busied themselves unpacking the medications and setting up the pharmacy. June took her place with the filipina nurses at the triage desk.

"The nurses have already registered and examined forty-five patients. Shall we register more?" Pastor Apura was indicating the long line of filipinos waiting outside the church. I walked outside. A slight drizzle began to fall. There were older, stooped women, and thin, frail old men. Children, some in rags without shoes, looked up at me with some trepidation. Most, however, raised their eyebrows in typical filipino greeting and demonstrated toothless smiles.

"Register more. But try not to register too far ahead of us." How could I turn these away? They had come so far, most by foot from the surrounding mountains. I could not disappoint them despite our jet-lag and the late afternoon hour.

Ninety patients later, we could go no farther. It had been a long day. Fatigue had settled heavily upon us all.

After a short rest and delicious meal at Pastor Bobby's home, we returned to the church. Pastor Apura had been showing a Gospel film. All were tired. I had even fallen asleep at Pastor Bobby's home.

I recognized my name in the midst of the island dialect as Pastor Apura introduced me. I slowly walked to the front and gave my testimony. Because of my fatigue, my words were quick and to the point. Within five to ten minutes, we were praying for the sick. Earlier in the day, seventy-nine of the ninety who came for medical attention had given their lives to Christ. Now I was just trying to make it through my fatigue to the end of my part of the service. An old woman hobbled to the front with two men assisting her. I prayed. I turned to leave.

"She felt something!" One of the men assisting the woman stopped me with these words.

"Tell her to do something she couldn't do before", I said.

She took several steps. Many rejoiced. Even though her steps were halting and unsteady, she made them on her own, something she had not been able to do in a long time.

Two nights in a row, I had been exhausted. Two nights in a row, the Holy Ghost demonstrated His presence with signs and miracles. I am glad that Jesus, the Everlasting God, the Lord, the Creator of heaven and earth, fainteth not, neither is He weary.

4 JUNE

"Telephone, sir!"

I was in the middle of my papaya and pineapple juice. The waitress had directed me to the South Seas Hotel front desk to the only working phone.

"Hello?"

"Dr. Price? This is Norma. How did you sleep?"

"Very well, how about you?"

"We didn't get back until midnight. We had another flat tire."

I felt so bad. We had departed in the car and had arrived back at the hotel well before 10PM. I knew how tired Norma and the rest were when we left them. I could only imagine how tired they must have been while they waited in the black Philippine night as the tire was repaired.

"But we are ready for today's clinic!"

I couldn't ask for a better group. Always ready to go without complaint.

Two hundred thirteen patients would be seen in the clinic, held in a local elementary school. Midway through these patients I noticed Dr. Maria Guese (Tess) examining a hydrocephalic child. Tess had just completed her pediatric specialty training at University of Santo Tomas and had graciously volunteered to accompany us to the islands from her home near Manila. (Miraculously, God provided the funds for all her expenses.) The child's head was grossly enlarged, appearing like a beachball with facial features. Tess and I knew it was just a matter of time before the retained water compressed his shrinking brain and spinal cord to the critical point causing death. His mother and grandmother gently cradled his enlarged head in their arms; despair deeply lining their faces.

Tess related the child's circumstances. Shortly after birth, his parents had been advised that he should have the necessary surgery to prevent hydrocephalus. However, they had no money. Subsequently, fluid accumulated within his skull as predicted. Now, the brain damage was irreversible. Sue, Norma and I prayed for his deliverance. Others gathered around in agreement.

Currently, there is a great political debate whether a health care crisis exists in the USA. In the Philippines, there is no debate. The crisis is real.

"Jesus said, 'In this world you shall have tribulation, but be of good cheer, for I have overcome the world'...." As I spoke these words, I considered the tribulation we had witnessed that very day in the clinic. Many were sick and diseased, not to mention the hydrocephalic child. My audience that evening consisted of mostly boys and girls that had gathered in the schoolyard to watch gospel films. Most of their parents failed to attend due to their interest in an important local basketball game. Rain began to pelt the children as they listened and the wind began to blow. Despite these hindrances, most of the seventy-five to one hundred children accepted Jesus as Lord under the shelter of the schoolhouse veranda; realizing the game of life to be eternal, and not temporal. We do not regard their heartfelt decisions as childish fantasies, but as the foundations for the rest of their lives. For them, as well as for the pathetic hydrocephalic little boy, we are expecting our prayers to our God in their behalf to make a significant difference.

5 JUNE

I have been to many worship services around the world. Many are in traditional church buildings with lofty spires, gothic stained glass windows, beautifully carved moldings and pews with plush cushions. I have also been to less traditional houses of worship. In Nepal I had been in an upper room of a stable. A Bulgarian congregation rented a municipal theater. In the USA I have been in services held in basketball stadiums, roller skating rinks, warehouses, automobile dealerships, schools and opera houses. A very famous church in Houston, Texas began in an old feed barn.

Pastor Gordon Apura's congregation meets in a tavern.

As I began to share on the platform in Pastor Apura's 'tavern', I glanced to my left. The tavern's daily menu on the east wall listed San Miguel beer, rum coke, daquiri, and other spirits.

That day, we served up a different spirit! It is true that God has poured out His Spirit upon all flesh. This Spirit heals, sets free, encourages and delivers! The setting is inconsequential.

"When can you come?" These words interrupted me as I was greeting various filipinos immediately after the service. Pastor Rizzy Montes with Norma at his side was imploring me to come to yet another needy area in the Philippines. Norma had introduced him to me earlier during the service.

"...Pastor Montes oversees eighty-two churches across Samar and surrounding islands," she said.

"That is wonderful!", I responded. He, his wife and daughter surrounded my wife and I. Their smiles were infectious; their spirit endearing. He offered his hand. As I took it, he bowed slightly in respect. Yet my respect for him and his family was about to grow immensely in the next few moments.

Norma continued, "They have traveled two days just to meet you!"

With his eyes penetrating, he asked again, "When can you come?"

Surely, I thought, there must be some other reason for his traveling for two days: perhaps another meeting.

"When can you come?" he asked once again.

"When's the best time to come?" I answered.

"Come anytime." he said.

I laughed. His persistence was admirable. I looked at Sue. She looked at me. I looked at Norma. She looked at me. I returned my gaze to Rizzy, only to hear again, "When can you come?"

I explained that many ask us, but we always pray about each and every invitation. "...a long time ago", I continued, I learned not to go in my own strength, nor in my own timing, but only when the Holy Ghost directs. If it was up to me, I would go everywhere and be gone ministering to the needy all the time. But only God knows the perfect timing and the perfect place. And when He directs, His Spirit moves which is much better than all the medication in the world!"

His response was, "Okay. But when can you come?"

I again turned to my wife and Norma. By now, Roberto was also with us. He, too, was feeling the intensity of this man of God.

Rizzy added, "You see, many in my place are sick. They have no means to buy the medicines prescribed by the doctor. They can see the doctor for free, but it's the medicines that cannot be afforded. Most are poor farmers, or fishermen. Most also do not know about God nor His promises. Most will not come to church. But they will if you come."

He paused as if to catch his breath. I could picture the suffering that he described. I also knew about the parasitic worm called schistosomiasis that afflicted Samar, attacking usually children and resulting in a horrible death at a young age. I also knew that we had in our possession the very medication to eradicate this disease. "So when can you come?", he asked once again.

Sue and Norma each made further inquiries. Eventually he revealed that the best time would be in February and that his many sons, who serve God as pastors, could assist me in every way. We also discovered that multiple small islands near Samar have no medical work of any kind, and no Christian witness. He suggested we go from island to island.

We walked down together the one flight of stairs to the dusty street below. As we descended, I advised, "If you truly want us to come, ask God to send us."

We all watched as he, his wife and daughter caught a pedicab. They all sat down and turned back to gaze toward us one last time. "They're going to the pier to catch a boat back to Cebu." Norma was whispering above the noise of the street. "From there, they will catch another boat for Calbayog, Samar, where they live."

"So they really came only to ask me to come?"

"Only for that reason," she answered, "two days here, and then two days back.

"He's not going to take 'no' for an answer", Sue said.

"I know. And now, he will ask God."

En route down the coast to the clinic that afternoon in Zamboanguita, the van suffered another flat. The delay was but temporary. Ninety-seven patients received medical attention. Seventy-six of these accepted Jesus as Lord. These were great victories. Yet I kept remembering, 'When can you come?'. I wondered also what the Holy Ghost would do about it.

6 JUNE

"How many are registered so far?", I asked.

Pastor Jerry responded, "Ninety." Pastor Jerry Vasquez was a member of a team of ministers and nurses sent by Pastor Tom O'Dowd from Word for the World Christian Fellowship, Bacolod City, Negros Occidental. Pastor Apura had asked for Pastor O'Dowd's assistance when we had initially confirmed our team's participation. Their travel from the other side of the island likely was fraught with hardships. Yet they came with joy in their hearts. Quickly the Holy Ghost melded us together. Their experience was greatly needed and appreciated, making our job so much easier.

I quickly went to each station to determine how everyone was holding up. Over the previous four days we had been working in the heat and humidity as well as participating in evangelistic and healing crusades. I could tell everyone needed some rest and relaxation.

I returned to Pastor Jerry and advised him to hold steady. "Don't register anymore but we may be able to resume once we catch up." I had said.

A few minutes later Pastor Apura approached me. "Doctor Price?", he began. As usual, his tone was filled with respect. "Could we consider seeing just a few more? There are those who have traveled all morning from the mountains and are just now arriving."

I glanced over to the doorway of the schoolhouse where we were conducting our examinations. It was jammed with bedraggled grandmothers, exhausted mothers and their tired children. Many were coughing. Some had open sores. How could I deny those who were suffering and had travelled so far?

One hundred twenty five patients would eventually be examined and provided free medication that day in Dauin. Success is not measured in numbers but in doing exactly what God has asked (in other words, obedience is greater than sacrifice). Nevertheless, our numbers indicated that one hundred eleven of these received Jesus.

Afterwards I looked at my tired team. I approached Norma. "Perhaps we could rent a boat and go over to Apo Island?"

Norma rushed over to determine the feasibility. We were to return to the city square in Dauin that evening for yet another evangelistic and healing crusade and it was already afternoon.

After a late lunch we found ourselves bumping along a mud and water filled path towards the beach at Zamboanguita. Our journey to Apo was estimated to be feasible.

The wooden boat was of local construction. Bamboo outrigging was affixed on both sides via rattan straps. There were no seats, only a wooden plank covering a motor in the bowels of the single-hull boat. Once we had all waded through the rocks and surf to board, a flimsy string was manipulated by a boatman to bring the motor to life. Another boatman in a blue cap and faded red cotton shirt held the rudder. There were thirteen of us huddled together on the top of the boat. I was at the bow, taking the brunt of the surf with each wave. Within a few seconds our street clothes were soaked with salt water.

I had been on these type of boats before. It therefore never occurred to me that the others may be a bit nervous. Granted, several could not swim, two small children were aboard, there were treacherous currents, no life vests and reportedly many sharks. But I was simply enjoying the ride.

To the south, the distant azure shadowy peaks of Mindanao on the horizon contrasted with the white fluffy clouds hanging in the deep blue sky. Siquijor with its coconut palms and patches of cogan grass was closer to the north. To the west was the shore of Negros which we had just abandoned. Coconut palms, towering above the beach, swayed with the breeze. Nothing, not even the intermittent screams of those in the boat, interrupted my revelry. I glanced at Sue sitting on the opposite end of the boat. She too was basking in enjoyment. My prayer at that moment was to return to these islands to spread the

Gospel of Jesus Christ, no matter what the cost. The islands were beautiful to my eyes. But it was the people which these islands held that tugged at my heart.

"Jesus said to the man, 'Don't be afraid, only believe'." I was in the Dauin city square. Hundreds had gathered to hear as I was beginning to share about Christ's ever-present healing power. We had survived the ride to and from Apo. It was especially exciting when the motor sputtered to a stop on our return. However, the boatmen nonchalantly connected the motor to a reserve fuel tank and the motor returned to life.

Soon, Sue, Norma, Roberto, Pastor Apura, his coworkers and I were surrounded by the hundreds in the dark moonless night praying for healing, forgiveness and deliverance. Many received, as evidenced by their profuse tears.

7 JUNE

"Now, the hard part begins." Pastor Apura was saying as we stood in the airport terminal awaiting our flight to Cebu. It was true. We had seen five hundred twenty five patients during our four days in Negros. Four hundred nine of these accepted Jesus as savior. Now it would be his job to ensure that all would receive the appropriate follow up and discipling.

"Truly, it has been our privilege to both meet and work with you. Our prayers will be continually with you."

Sue, Norma and Roberto added their accolades to my words. We had seen a man of great vision and organization during our days with him. He also possessed a humble spirit, was not afraid to work hard nor ask for help when necessary.

"Dr. Price, are you thinking about a medical outreach on Apo?", he asked. "As you know, everything must be brought in to Apo from Negros and there is no medical clinic, nor even a pharmacy on the entire island."

"I'm not only thinking, but also praying."

Well, when you return next year....", he paused and smiled. I had not yet committed to return which he well knew.

"You pray", I interrupted, "and when God sends us, we will have a mighty influence for good and for God on Apo!"

One last embrace and we abandoned the shelter of the terminal. The morning sun was already cooking the tarmac as we approached the Philippine Airlines turboprop.

The Fokker 50 rose quickly over the Mindanao Sea.

"Will we be coming back some day, Daddy?" Andrew was sitting beside me looking out the window through the morning mist at the island below.

"If God sends us", I answered.

Andrew turned to look me square in the face. His serious six year old brown eyes were filled with compassion "I sure hope He does", he said, "because those sick people really need our help."

My thoughts turned to the hundreds we had seen. Most had no other access to any type of medical care. The cost of the medication was simply too prohibitive. Many barely had sufficient funds for transportation to the existing medical clinics, much less for the prescribed medications. I thought especially of the hydrocephalic boy and others who were beyond hope simply because they did not have the funds at the time when medical assistance could have prevented their current predicament. Andrew was correct, those sick people needed our help. I am glad we came. I was confident also that our God would do something, because He is moved by the cries of His children. Remembering the filipinos' condition, I know there had been, and will continue to be, many cries.

The flight was uneventful, except for the usual two or three trips with Andrew to the restroom. I too, was fascinated by the funny blue water in the toilet. We soon landed at Cebu's Mactan International Airport, the very site where hundreds of years ago, Ferdinand Magellan spilled his blood and died at the hands of native heathen tribes.

After a change of planes in Cebu, we were on our way to Bohol, the site of another blood incident. Also hundreds of years ago, the spanish explorer Legaspi, who followed Magellan, struck a blood covenant with Rajah Sikatuna to ensure that neither he nor any of his men would suffer the same ignonimous fate. We would soon visit the very hill overlooking the sea where this blood covenant occurred.

We, however, were coming to testify of another blood covenant that took place on another hill. Even though the blood covenant struck by Jesus, God in the flesh, occurred thousands of years ago, and the specific hill was many of thousands of miles away, it is relevant for everyone. No one needs to suffer the same ignonimous fate as do those who are ignorant of Jesus Christ's selfless, heroic deed and deny His Lordship. Jesus' blood covenant guarantees peace for everyone everywhere.

Touchdown on the airstrip at Tagbilaran City was followed by the routine but vigorous procedures to slow the plane. We soon exited to be greeted again by an oven of hot humid air. We were also greeted by Dr. Rudy Trigo and his large delegation. After many shell necklaces and hugs we noticed the banner of welcome draped over the wooden fence near the terminal. This welcome was but a shadow of hospitality which would be bestowed upon us during our brief stay. Within minutes of our arrival, we were whisked away via jeepney. Soon we would again be in the midst of a very busy clinic.

Many from across Bohol and other nearby smaller islands heard of our free clinics via radio, newspaper and several banners erected at strategic locations. Dr. Trigo had utilized his resources to ensure us of an excellent turnout. He had also mobilized his pastors and evangelists to assist us. Over one hundred patients were already registered and had been waiting in the church since early morning. Many had travelled as far as one hundred kilometers, spending precious money that would have otherwise been used to feed their families.

Rudy had established March of Faith in Tagbilaran City years ago. Over the past several decades, he has been a positive force throughout not only Bohol, but the entire region. His influence extends beyond what would normally be expected of a pastor. He once suggested to the mayor that local pedicabs be allowed to exhibit scripture. Thereafter, by mayoral decree, all pedicabs were not only allowed, but required to clearly display a Bible verse.

In addition to over two hundred self supporting churches, he has several evangelistic teams on the islands of Bohol, Samar, and Mindanao. These teams conduct crusades for three weeks out of every month. If he senses a need, he fills it, as was repeatedly demonstrated during our medical outreach. He also does not keep filipino time; when he says 7:00 PM, he doesn't mean 7:45 PM.

As we were seeing patients in the church, Dr. Trigo marvelled at the scores of people he had never seen before. This was evidently significant for a man who had been established in the ministry for years. He knew many in Tagbilaran City. Few to him were strangers. Except of course the patients he was now seeing in his church because of the medical clinic.

Vicente, my interpreter, was relating the chief complaint of a man sitting across the desk from me. It was obvious that there was little I could do medically for him. He had suffered a stroke years ago resulting in right sided weakness. He also had hypertension and diabetes.

"Tell him we will give him some medication for his problems, but we do not have anything that will restore his strength."

Vicente began to interpret, but I interrupted him. "But tell him about Jesus."

Vicente turned again to the thin old man. I let my head fall, wishing there was something more I could do. I also began to wonder whether the numbers of those reportedly saved were true. There had been such a great response that I was beginning to doubt the validity of such numbers. I looked at the papers on my desk. Vicente was still talking.

The old man then began to repeat Vicente's words. It was then when I saw his tears hit my papers. I looked up from where I was sitting into his bloodshot eyes as he accepted Christ.

The old man turned to me as he was leaving. "Praise the Lord, Doctor, praise the Lord!" His tears had not yet dried. His eyes were still bloodshot. Yet there was a sense of joy that was absent before.

I decided to doubt the numbers no more.

8 JUNE

It was past midday. The low latitude tropical sun was beating down upon the church. Across the room I could see Tess wiping her brow. It had been a long morning. We had seen one hundred ninety one patients. The portable air conditioner in the corner of the room could do little with the patients constantly moving in and out with the door open.

Among these was a sixty eight year old female complaining of a "sore" in her mouth. When I asked her to open her mouth I found to my horror a mass of tumor which completely filled her oral cavity. The angry red tissue was full of abscesses and fistulas percolating with pus. I gave her some medications but also suggested she believe God for the miracle she needed.

A four year old girl also had "mouth problems". Her problem, however was not as horrific. Her teeth had simply rotted away to irregular stumps surrounded by inflamed gums. Unfortunately, this was all too common among people of all ages, doubtless contributing to widespread malnutrition and its associated diseases.

Another woman, fifty seven, but appearing much older, was suffering from a uterine leiomyoma. She described her pain and bleeding episodes as unbearable. But she gladly received Jesus with many tears right at my desk. I am believing that she also will receive a miraculous healing touch, another benefit of our Lord Jesus Christ.

I don't have to wonder about the sixty six year old man who was deaf. After prayer, he could hear!

"He wants us to come back after lunch."

"He wants us to do what?!" I asked incredulously.

After one hundred ninety one patients, we were all tired. Throughout the morning, I periodically checked on the others. Tess, as indicated previously, had been working nonstop. Because she spoke the dialect, many patients asked her a multitude of exhausting questions.

From early morning, June had been surrounded by hordes of sick filipinos as she attempted to record their current complaints in detail. The hard wooden chair in the stifling heat surrounded by warm sick bodies obviously was taxing at the least.

Norma and Roberto had been extremely busy all morning counting, labeling and sorting various medications. Most patients received more than one prescription which multiplied their work three to four fold. Norma also served as my liaison with the filipino volunteers.

Agnes carefully explained the necessity and administration as she dispensed each medication. Commonly I would see her utilize diagrams of kidneys and other body systems, expending additional energy to ensure that all understood.

Sue was wherever I wanted her. Most of the time she assisted Norma and Roberto. However, when a problem arose anywhere, I called upon her to correct it.

(God could not have provided a better group of individuals. Each paid their own way and sacrificed greatly for the privilege of sweating here amongst sick people they didn't even know. They also forfeited vacation time they could have easily spent with their families.)

Therefore, when Norma advised me that Dr. Trigo wanted us to come back for further punishment that very afternoon I was a bit dismayed. We had been working extremely hard to provide care for a quantity of patients that would have taken weeks back in the USA. This would be our sixth day straight without a break. The sometime overwhelming numbers in conjunction with the magnitude of their suffering was enough to break each of our hearts a hundred times over. Everyone was exhausted and looking forward to much needed rest before our return that evening.

"Can't they come back tomorrow?" I continued. "Explain to him that we have already examined over one hundred ninety patients."

Norma left to relay my message. In her absence, Agnes, Tess and Roberto had joined Sue and I near the small wooden table where the medications had been dispensed that day. All were anticipating rest and relaxation.

Norma soon reappeared. "He said that you can stop if you want, but there is a group of patients that have travelled over one hundred kilometers, which took them eight hours. They have spent money sacrificially to get here: that is, food money. They also have no place to spend the night. If you do not see them, they will be forced to return home still sick."

The small group was silent. I sensed all eyes upon me. Looking down at my feet sheepishly, I realized our fatigue paled in comparison to the struggles and severe hardships these unfortunate filipinos had endured to come.

I heard myself reply, "We'll break for lunch and then return to see the rest."

That day, one hundred seventy nine of the two hundred forty patients examined received Jesus Christ as Savior. We were all glad that we stayed.

"...all who desire to be healed, stand up and come forward, and God will heal you." As Dr. Trigo interpreted my final statement of the evening service, I considered what I had just uttered. It was admittedly quite a statement for a physician.

The crowd was not very large, perhaps one hundred to one hundred fifty. But soon fifteen to twenty people were standing near the front. I declared a simple prayer of healing, reminding God of His Word, the devil of his defeat, and each of us of our authority in Christ Jesus. I then laid my hands on each as I simultaneously declared, "In the name of Jesus, be healed!"

I went to my seat, but rose again to my feet when the testimonies began. A woman received relief of chest pain from which she had suffered for years. Others were also miraculously pain free (a major miracle in a country where even tylenol was too expensive for the normal people). Three filipinos who could each barely see before I prayed, could now see without difficulty. My statement was true. All who desired healing that night, received.

The joy of the Lord was truly present. Soon after everyone calmed down, I escorted my sons, Andrew and Austin, to the front. They were holding in their little hands copies of my book, "FREEDOM FROM PAIN". Immediately, they were mobbed. Many were reaching simultaneously, knocking the books to the floor where they were quickly confiscated by the crowd.

Andrew turned to me and whispered something. At first I didn't hear so I leaned close as I picked him up in my arms. "Daddy", he whispered in my ear, "they're just like hungry goats!"

At first, I didn't understand. But then I recalled a few months earlier when I had taken both Andrew and Austin to the petting zoo at the Houston Livestock Show and Rodeo. We bought some food and fed it to the goats who quickly knocked the cup of food to the ground and devoured every last pellet in seconds.

I whispered back, "Yes, Andrew. They are just like hungry goats."

We unfolded the side flaps on the jeepney. The night drizzle gently pelted the Tagbilaran streets as we made our way to Dr. Trigo's house. We were soon roaring up his long driveway on the side of the hill. After maneuvering past the curve we were soon under the carport.

Inside, the table was already set. As we were seated, steaming mounds of chicken adobo, pork filled lumpia, vegetable pancit, pineapple, mangos, jackfruit and the ubiquitous rice were strategically placed amongst our table settings. I made sure that my favorite, fried bananas, were within my reach. Andrew had fallen asleep in the jeepney and was now dozing on the couch. Our younger son Austin, however, was wide awake. As usual, when food was available, he also made himself available.

As we were enjoying the feast, Dr. Trigo began with noticeable excitement in his voice, "Tonight we saw God move in a way I had never seen before. Everyone who came forward was healed! You prayed a simple prayer, and God answered!"

"Also, not only the poor and destitute are coming to your clinic. There is a man, a lawyer, a very influential lawyer, the one in charge of the licensing agency here in Bohol."

"The licensing agency?" I questioned.

"Yes. He is the one who approves all the licenses, whether they be to operate a jeepney, pedicab or even to establish a new business. Well, I have known him for years. And for years I have been inviting him to come to my church. But he never came. Today he came. He was examined by you; he and his whole family, a wife and two grown daughters. And he accepted Jesus today; he and his whole family."

He paused, and then continued with noticeable enthusiasm in his voice. "For years I have been inviting him to my church. Now, you have been here only two days and he came to church. Had you not offered your medical ministry, he likely would have never heard the true Gospel."

"I am seeing people in my church that I had never seen before: people that probably would never ever have entered a church except for your medical clinics. My pastors and evangelists are complaining that they have never prayed for so many people in one day before. As they stand bent over, they are getting backaches." Rudy paused and laughed. "But they are so excited. Many churches will be established because of your visit because so many have come from so far. There is even a woman who came from Dipolog City."

"Dipolog City?!" Norma asked.

Everyone looked at each other. We all knew Dipolog City was on the western part of Mindanao, a good two to three days boat ride.

"Yes. I announced that you would be providing free medical examinations on my radio program. This response has shown me that we can reach those that we could never reach in any other way."

As I listened, I cut into my fifth banana. I had waited seven long years for these and was determined to enjoy as many as my stomach could hold.

"The Bible says , 'Go into all the world and preach to every creature'. Every creature has a family and every family has someone who is sick." Dr. Trigo paused. Tears were in his eyes. "My dream is that every family in these islands hear the true Gospel. Not a watered down version but a Gospel that can be used to fight the battles of this life on a daily basis."

As he was speaking, I recalled how most filipinos, though they may go to a catholic or protestant church, utilize animistic remedies for life's day to day problems.

"We hope that God will send you back to us. We can go up into the chocolate hills, or even to the islands of Samar or Mindanao. Your medical exams will draw filipinos from across these islands to Christ!"

Then I recalled Andrew's words once more, 'Daddy, they're just like hungry goats!'.

9 JUNE

The late afternoon sun hung precariously amongst the gathering storm clouds. My position in the very back of the jeepney enroute to the airport magnified the many bumps and potholes in the rugged road. A few years previously, bumps such as these would have precipitated severe pain in my diseased hip. However, God healed me and today I was simply enjoying the ride. I also revelled in the thought of what we had accomplished on this the seventh and last day of clinics. It was the busiest day of all. Two hundred forty five received medical treatment.

Three patients stood out in my memory. Two little sisters, ages four and six, had impetigo so bad that their legs from the knees down were totally encased with pus and yellow scabs. Another woman had been born with neurofibromatosis. Her left leg was consequentially five to six times the size of her right one. Through an interpreter, I indicated that the God who healed my leg could do the same for them.

The jeepney rolled to a stop. We entered the small terminal through the open west side. It looked more like a garage than an airport. Security guards required that each of our checked bags be opened. The security personnel were soon satisfied. We then hauled our luggage to the counter. After considerable bantering back and forth amongst our filipino hosts and the employees of Philippine Airlines, Dr. Trigo arrived. Quickly Dr. Trigo, Roberto and I were back in the air conditioned office of the airport director's office. Whatever the problem, if there was a problem, it apparently was resolved. Boarding passes in hand, we headed towards the departure lounge.

"Dr. Price, let me show you our island."

Rudy led me to a large map on the south wall of the terminal. Indicating a faded area on the bottom left, he said, "This is Tagbilaran City. And way over here..." He walked to his right and on his tip toes pointed to a small island on the very opposite side of the map. "This is Lapinin, the island from which those patients had travelled all day to see you. The ones you came back for."

I followed his finger as he traced their most likely route. "Probably they took a small boat to the mainland and spent the night here. And then they took a bus to here." He indicated a small village on the southern Bohol coast. "From there they likely waited for a jeepney to take them the rest of the way."

Recollections of the dusty, rocky roads filled my mind. I was both pleased and relieved that we had stayed. The effort these people underwent to travel such roads in cramped, hot buses and jeepneys must have been excessive.

"And here, amongst the chocolate hills...," He paused as he pointed to Carmen in the very center of Bohol, "...is where we can set up our next medical outreach."

When he turned to look at my response he was smiling broadly.

"We, of course, are praying for your quick return."

Soon we were airborne. Once again I was sitting beside Andrew in a Philippine Airlines Fokker 50 turboprop. We watched the wheels retract into the wing. The blue sea below was littered with hundreds of green islands. Some were mountainous. Others were flat coral reefs. But all had people: likely desperate, sick, and destitute. Most had no knowledge of a loving creator God who wanted a personal relationship with each. Most also did not know that He wanted them all to have freedom from pain, just as He had provided me.

Sue, who was sitting across the aisle, nudged me and asked, "Are you ready to leave the Philippines?"

I turned again to view the islands. We had dispensed over thirty four thousand tablets of various types in treating one thousand one hundred fifty nine patients. Eight hundred seventy eight of these accepted Jesus Christ in the clinics. Others had received miraculous healings via that Name. I would later learn that the old man from our very first service who I assumed to be hopelessly crippled and aphasic was talking and moving his arms (my medical mind had told me such would be impossible). Untold others accepted Jesus in the nightly evangelistic meetings.

Then I recalled those with impetigo, malnutrition, boils, purulent coughs, open sores, skin rashes, weakness, diarrhea and other afflictions. I looked at my wife and two boys sitting with me on the plane. They were well dressed, well nourished and were in excellent health. I wondered what I would do if they had any of the plagues we had just treated and I had no means to help them. I wondered also what I would do if I had no knowledge of the loving heavenly Father made personal by the heroic deeds of Jesus Christ.

I would hope that someone somewhere would come help me.

I, too, would get on a boat and travel as many days as it took to ask someone, 'When can you come?'. I would also be as hungry for news of a loving God that I, too, would be like a 'hungry goat'.

I turned to Sue. "We came and did what we could do. Then we watched the Holy Ghost do the rest. I'm ready to leave."

After a pause, I added, "I'm also ready for the next time."

18 OCT

The constant drone of the big engines abruptly changed and the pitch of the 747-300 shifted. We had begun our decent through the rough Indian skies to Indira Ghandi International Airport. Eight hours on Air France flight 184 had made us both anxious to regain our land legs.

Outside there was only black darkness.

The normal rotation of the earth had long ago forced the sun below the horizon, but the Indian night was made even darker by the cries of the infirm, sick, and dying. Bubonic plague, and most recently the pneumonic variety, aptly described as the black death, cursed the land. Other diseases bred freely. Within the next week, malignant cerebral malaria, which I knew as Plasmodium falciparum, would claim over 240 more lives. Experts at a recent AIDS conference (Yokohoma, Japan) had predicted over 10 million AIDS cases, the modern day plague, within India's borders by the end of the decade.

As we peered through the window, Sue and I could see the faded yellow lights of the land below through the clouds of dust and wood smoke. Landfall was approaching. Fifteen years had passed since Sue had spent several months here. My last trip was more recent. We had both seen the result of spiritual wickedness up close: I in temporary medical clinics for the indigent, Sue in orphanages for the castaways. We could only imagine the misery and torment that permeated every aspect of human existence.

Touchdown was surprisingly smooth. Clearance through customs was not. At 2:00 A.M., we finally ventured through the green pathway into the arrival hall. Outside, masses of Indians lined the restraining wall like bacteria on an agar plate.

"Dr. Price!" I turned to see Abby in the midst of the multitude. We managed to rendezvous outside.

In the car, Sue and I sat in silence. The hours of flying, late hour and the time zone change were beginning to catch up to us. Outside, we both saw the dusty road lined with an assortment of simple structures including teastalls, and crude cement block dwellings. The pale dim streetlights seemed to be losing the battle against the ubiquitous darkness. Or perhaps our tired eyes made the night seem like molasses. Nevertheless, we could discern sporadic groups of men in their traditional dhotis, stained by the grime and faded by the years, lying by the roadside. Some slept on the ground, others on the tables used in the daytime to hawk their wares. Entire families could also be seen huddled together on the dirt and doorsteps. Those on a doorstep, I knew, felt fortunate for the shelter it provided. Had we been able to get closer, we would have been able to hear the rattle of tuberculosis, smell the sour stench of typhoid fever, and see the destruction wrought by legions of other diseases and infestations. Big trucks in need of mufflers and belching black smoke couldn't even elicit a glance from these slumberers, despite their close proximity and blaring passage.

Cows, an object of worship, roamed unmolested, munching from piles of garbage and refuse. This refuse also nourished the rats which were also worshiped and sometimes even fed in special temples. In this country of close to a billion people, there were also approximately 10 billion rats. The rats harbored the fleas. Within the fleas the dreaded <u>Yersinia pestis</u> swarmed, waiting for an opportunity which would lead to the black death that the newspapers reported as the plague.

Our car turned into the hotel driveway. Once in our room, I turned to Sue.

"Well." I began, "what do you think?"

"Nothing has changed," she replied with exhaustion in her voice, "nothing has changed in fifteen years."

And probably, I thought, for centuries.

19 OCT

"Jesus will give you peace in your heart and health to your body...." Pastor Osteen preached with boldness from Hebrews 13:8. The public address system echoed off the concrete columns as his words, the Word of God, reverberated across the crowd in excess of forty-five thousand. Most were sitting Indian style with legs crossed on the cricket fields inside the running track of Jawaharlal Nehru Stadium.

As we had approached the sports complex earlier, I had been amazed at the sheer size. Massive steel girders shot into the sky at each corner, hoisting the beacons that illuminated the night. This blaze of brightness could be seen for miles, despite the ever present Delhi dust, smoke, haze, and darkness. The closer we came, the imposing outside walls loomed ever higher. Once inside, I imagined the mammoth structure considered us as insects. Great concrete pillars towered above the field and gracefully sloped upward. From our position, only the Indian night immediately above the field could be seen, all other surrounding structures had been blotted out by the stadium's massive edifice.

Earlier, our car had maneuvered amongst streams of people swarming into the entryways like ants heading for a pile of sugar. This multitude appeared despite the advertising ban. I remembered turning to Pastor Osteen, who was sitting close by in the back seat and asking, "Are you ready?" His answer was written on his face. God had made him ready for that very moment.

"Jesus is a God of love: He will heal and deliver! You do not need to stay sick. Many things change: politics, educational institutions, people. But Jesus never changes. He is the same yesterday, today and forever!"

Sue and I were in the midst of the crowd as we heard his words interrupted only by that of Brother Martin, his interpreter. A pin could have been heard had it been dropped; so engrossed was the crowd. I don't believe any of us, even Pastor Osteen, realized at that moment the miracle that was occurring. We were in New Delhi, the capital city of a heathen land in a stadium that by law was prohibited to be used for religious services of any kind. Later, P. G. Vargis, who had arranged the meetings, would explain how this law was abrogated. "I simply told them that this was not a religious meeting, but a healing one! Only then did they agree and sign the appropriate documents." This occurred only hours before the meetings were to begin! God had pulled down man-made laws for His purpose.

Suddenly, two of the four great beams of light hanging above us went out. Yet the people remained attentive. Only we westerners, who were not accustomed to frequent brown-outs, seemed distracted. Soon, another of the lights went dark, leaving only one to shine. Yet the one was sufficient to bring us to God's demonstration of His presence.

John Greiner, whose vantage point was on the platform behind Pastor Osteen as he preached, described it as a rush of wind that filtered down from the top of the enormous stadium through the midst of the people, prompting the masses to run forward. The power of such was so great, he had later reported, that others on the platform could but bow their heads and weep.

Over one hundred received healing of deafness that very night. Among these, was a man from Orissa who had been completely deaf, untouched by doctors, for twenty-four years. Another who testified, was a woman who lost her hearing at age ten. Tonight, at age sixty, she could finally hear clearly!

Only one light beam overhead remained operational. Yet, suddenly the Indian sky wasn't quite so dark.

20 OCT

"Where is he? It's way past 9:30."

We had arrived downstairs to find John and Pastor Osteen contemplating the tardiness of our driver. The morning session with the pastors was likely already in full swing, yet our transportation had not yet materialized.

"Maybe he got tied up in traffic after taking Joel in earlier." John was referring to Joel Osteen who planned an earlier departure in order to get some video shots of Talkadora Auditorium.

I surveyed the usual chaos of the front hotel entrance. People of various colors and nationalities busily scurried in and out. Several ladies were dressed elegantly in traditional saris. A scotsman hurriedly walked past in his kilt. Another gentleman, evidently a Sikh, wore a finely tailored suit that only enhanced his carefully adjusted turban. Others were dressed in less refined clothing. All were focused on their day's itinerary.

We were also focused. Therefore, we were slightly anxious regarding our absentee driver.

Suddenly, John exclaimed, "There's Joel now!"

Joel was extricating himself from a black taxi. As he was retrieving his video equipment from the trunk, he spotted us. Soon we discovered that Chandra, our driver, never showed. Rather than wait, Joel hired a taxi. However, despite careful instructions, Talkadora Auditorium proved to be much too elusive for that particular driver.

Turning to the doorman for assistance, Pastor Osteen soon had another taxi and we all piled in. After much Hindi jabbering, in which we repeatedly heard the word, 'Talkadora', the doorman assured us of our 'safe delivery' to the much named auditorium.

As we ventured out into New Delhi traffic, I contemplated the doorman's choice of words. Our taxi seemed very vulnerable as we darted among the ubiquitous pedicabs, soot-belching buses, rattling cars and the rumbling heavy trucks. Oftentimes the latter would almost be upon us when our driver would nonchalantly accelerate at the last minute, seemingly oblivious to any impending danger. I had been in much more harried traffic situations, but 'safe delivery' remained a major statement of faith.

Talkadora Auditorium was set back away from the street in a park-like setting. Our driver maneuvered through the iron gate to park just outside the main entrance. As we exited the car, an uncanny silence, atypical for an Asian metropolis, greeted our ears. Obviously, the many trees and shrubs surrounding the auditorium buffered the sounds of the city.

Soon, however, a new sound could be heard: a sound of praises to our God. As the doors of the auditorium were opened, the muffled sounds of praise exploded into a welcome crescendo. The wooden floor was lined with rows and rows of empty seats; their occupants stood close by singing praises to God. Along the periphery were multiple levels of seats that rose to the very ceiling. All were similarly occupied with Indians in a variety of dress; saris, dhotis, sulwar quartas, pajamas, clerical robes and even western style suit and ties. Sue and I took our place on the floor. All around us, the three thousand five hundred plus pastors filled the building to the very rafters. All were singing joyfully unto the Lord; some with heads bowed and eyes closed, others with eyes open looking up as to heaven with arms outstretched.

Gradually, these praises ceased, allowing for preliminary introductions and the opening prayer by the designated chairman of the morning's meetings.

Pastor Osteen began with a strong declaration from the book of Daniel, "They that do know their God shall be strong and do exploits!" As he subsequently expounded the scriptures concerning the 'spirit man' that is within each of us, I turned to see the faces of the audience. Behind the multiple cameras spread around the meeting hall, as well as behind the audio-video controls, were the faces of several turbaned Sikhs. They had the intent faces of those hired to record these proceedings. Today their expressions showed little comprehension. In the days ahead I would detect a noticeable change, even in the gruff exterior of the large, heavy-set Sikh who was obviously in charge. But today their faces revealed little insight.

On the contrary were the faces of the pastors and evangelists. Their's were ones that announced pure joy, excitement, and even amazement as they drank in all they could.

This enthusiasm only grew as Pastor Osteen explained each point.

"It is your spirit man...that God saves and gives eternal life...to which God communicates...with which you exercise Bible faith...that Jesus makes righteous...." The only interruptions were those spontaneous shouts of jubilation and worship from comprehending individuals.

Finally, he declared, "Jesus didn't tell the lost to go to the Church. He told the Church to go to the lost!" The response was an overwhelming thundering applause of hand clapping and voice cheering. Obviously, the 'spirit man' in everybody was responding to the evangelical call.

The ovation shook the very foundations as Pastor Osteen and John exited. Simultaneously, an elderly man in long white clerical robes, the dress of an Indian Methodist Bishop, abandoned his front seat on the floor to follow them. His ivory tunic had long ago faded, if indeed it had ever been pristine white. He was stooped somewhat along his thoracic vertebrae and his thinning black hair was streaked with gray. He overtook Pastor Osteen in the hallway just off the front foyer.

"Your words are life to me!" He exclaimed with tears moistening his weathered face. He bowed with respect, shook Pastor's hand, and then left.

Such a brief discourse yet one with great significance. I had seen his face, one that had been streaked with wrinkles of age and years of working for Christ in a very hard place. But this very same face revealed an encouraged, joyful heart.

That afternoon, Sue and I, after a quick lunch, lugged our bags of medicines back to the conference site to attend the sick among the attendees. We treated sixty-six; many with skin boils, chronic bronchitis, asthma, malaria, typhoid and even severe malnutrition. As each detailed their disease process and I examined their typically frail frame, I contemplated the severe hardships they faced in daily life. I wondered whether I would have the faith to endure in similar circumstances. It was our joy to treat these dedicated workers, thereby symbolically washing their feet. Our prayer was that by such efforts, we would enable these same feet to carry the Gospel of Peace to even more distant villages.

Evening came quickly. Dahta picked us up at the hotel for delivery to the stadium. He had replaced Chandra, our driver who had mysteriously disappeared that morning. Dahta revealed that Chandra's steering wheel had been forced into his chest after his car collided with an errant army truck; occurring only shortly after dropping us off the previous evening. The hospital had treated and released him but, needless to say, he was in no shape to drive.

Dahta was relating this story as he weaved in and out of other vehicles, causing all of us in the back seat to slide back and forth against each other. Silence prevailed as we all harbored a thankful heart for God's divine protection.

At the stadium, approximately seventy five thousand gathered under a full moon which hung low in the eastern sky. Evidently, word of the healings from the night before had gotten out. All were waiting with great expectancy.

P.G. Vargis turned to me as I sat on the platform, waving my book that was available in three different languages; English, Malayalam, and Hindi. He and his coworkers had labored many months to birth the crusade and the Pastor's Conference; a miracle in its own right considering the many denominations and even Catholic Church that cooperated in one spirit. Soon, I found myself behind the podium surveying a bigger crowd than I had ever seen in my life.

After a little hesitation, I began. "I am a physician certified by the American Board of Internal Medicine. I underwent many years of training to attain this certification, and subsequently received additional expertise in infectious diseases and tropical medicine. I have many certificates and diplomas that attest to this fact on my office wall."

Pausing with each phrase to allow Brother Martin to interpret, I continued. "But none of this training and not one of these diplomas nor certificates was able to help me when I developed an incurable disease, a degeneration of the hip."

"Only Jesus could help me."

This statement was greeted with incredulous silence.

I then elucidated some of the gory details of my ordeal, especially the pain and hopelessness of my ever walking normally again. As I spoke, I could sense the Holy Ghost urging me to provide a demonstration.

"Today, because of what Jesus did for me, I can walk, I can run, and I can jump. You, too, can receive your heart's desire. Listen to what Pastor Osteen says about this Jesus. If you really want healing, believe on Jesus, and you will get it!"

Pastor Osteen came up behind me and urged me to walk for the people to see. The Spirit came upon me and soon I was running around the stage; I suppose not too dignified for a physician. Yet it also wasn't too dignified for the King of the whole world to die nailed to a tree.

Pastor Osteen delivered his message of a loving God that sent His only Son, Jesus, to the sinners and ungodly. He talked about His suffering and His sacrifice on the cross. He talked about His blood. Then he revealed Jesus to be alive even today and that He still healed the sick. "...one touch from Jesus can cause all problems to vanish.... The things that are impossible with men are possible with God!"

At his invitation, thousands streamed towards the front. Others could not make it out of the aisles due to the sheer numbers. All confessed Jesus as Lord right where they stood.

While the masses came, I noticed a man hobbling forward with a walker off to the left of the platform. As I watched, I could see uncoordinated legs turned inward and his severe difficulty with every move. Each step was a struggle. I imagined nerve damage and severe atrophied muscles.

Moments later, a commotion arose to my right. This very same man was walking without the walker with hands stretched to the sky. His movements were not smooth, yet they were nothing like those of just a few moments previously. I know the critics would concentrate on his persistent weakness. But a baby doesn't suddenly jump up and start walking in one minute, or even in one day. It takes months to coordinate unused muscles. There was definitely a difference in his gait, especially since he was no longer leaning heavily on his walker.

He then told me, and then subsequently the entire crowd, that he had been in an automobile accident. He had lost his ability not only to walk, but also to talk. After a touch from Jesus, we witnessed him do both!

Many were weeping with joy as they received long denied healing. Most were cripples, some lame from birth. Little boys had withered limbs grow into normal legs before our very eyes! Others, including a nurse, would provide specific details about the power of God a few days later.

The crowd began to press forward. Some even made their way onto the platform, hungry for a touch from Jesus. Suddenly, a woman in the crowd began to shriek. Most of us turned to see her fall as if dead on the ground. The surrounding crowd separated quickly as she fell. A few of the ushers gradually made their way to her. Later we were told that she had been delivered from demonic powers.

More and more came onto the platform. It soon became apparent, by the erratic sway of the structure, that a quick departure would be in everyone's best interests.

"Grab onto me and don't let go!" I yelled to Sue as I simultaneously grasped her hand and headed towards the nearest ramp leading down to the car. At the ramp, we caught up with the others.

"Papa! Follow me!" P. G. Vargis shouted over the pandemonium to Pastor Osteen.

Later, I would reflect on this choice of words as Pastor Osteen related how he had first met Brother Vargis. "I found him living in a little one room hut in the foothills of the Himalayas: he, his wife and four children. He was struggling. Jesus led me to him...." His words trailed off as tears filled his eyes. Truly, the tears of a father, or, in this case, a 'Papa'.

I could picture the hut, for I, too, had been in the very town he spoke of. Katra was at the foothill of a Hindu shrine in Kashmir. I remembered the wickedness of the city. I had felt the demonic despair that penetrated life. I could imagine the difficulties and persecution Brother Vargis had faced. I knew his family had been treated like dirt.

But Pastor Osteen treated him like a son.

"Papa! Follow me!" He had said.

We all ducked down and followed Brother Vargis and his workers through the crowd. They formed a wedge, much like I imagined the famous flying horsemen of Notre Dame. With chaos all around, we wedged our way to the car and deposited ourselves in the back seat.

The car eased away from the crowd and soon exited the stadium.

Overhead, none of the lights had gone out as they had done the night before. But it was not the beams of these lights that had pierced the darkness that night. 'Papa' had revealed that the light of the world, Jesus Christ, was still alive!

21 OCT

We again were being ferried through Delhi traffic by Dahta at the usual rapid pace. Horns of various pitch and frequency filled the air. The smell of diesel smoke filtered in through the cracks in the window. The speed of our vehicle was much like those at Indianapolis on Memorial Day.

"Tell him that I want to get there, but in one piece." Papa was again giving his instructions to John. As John delivered the message from his seat in the front, Pastor Osteen added, "I want to go to heaven, but not necessarily today!"

Our greeting at Talkadora Auditorium was much like it had been the previous day, only more enthusiastic. All faces demonstrated exuberant smiles: joy was epidemic.

Fortunately, another epidemic that had threatened to cancel these very meetings, the pneumonic plague, was conspicuously absent. Later that day we would examine one hundred four of these pastors. None harbored the plague. Presently, as I Looked around at the cheerful faces, it was difficult to believe that such a contagion had forced the government to cancel public meetings and even schools. Only a few days before our arrival, this ban was lifted.

Instead, we were surrounded by a plague of jubilation. I noticed that even the Sikhs operating the video equipment were getting into the act as they nodded their heads rhythmically to the music. On stage, Brother Vargis hopped, only as he could, clapping his hands under lifted legs as he danced unto the Lord.

Shortly, Pastor Osteen began his discourse on confessing God's Word. "God wants us to have dominion in this life. In Genesis, God said, 'Let us make a man, somebody like ourselves, and let us give him dominion and be masters of all of life'."

Pastor Osteen continued to encourage his audience, referencing multiple scriptures throughout the Bible, both Old Testament and New.

"We are well able to take the land...but we must keep a positive confession. When you confess the Word, you confess God's words: you say what God says about the situation...Confession will bring you into possession! Just watch your words. Talk faith. Say what God says. Don't speak words to describe a situation. Speak words to change a situation!"

The ears of his listeners soaked up his words like hungry dogs gobble up biscuits. The more he spoke, the more they wanted. Their appetite for God's Word was as an unquenchable craving.

"All things are possible to those who believe. Your confession should be, 'I am a new creature...I have been delivered from the power of satan...I am redeemed from the curse of the law...I am blessed with the blessings of Abraham...I am more than a conqueror...I can do all things through Christ who strengthens me!'"

Immediately after the session ended, a middle-aged man, his face lined with distress, approached me. "Doctor, could you please see my friend's daughter? She has been sick for many months."

I stopped and turned to face him directly. His friend was at his side, obviously with little knowledge of English.

"How old is she and what are her symptoms?"

"She is in her early twenties." He answered. "She has had fever for a long time. Last night we took her to Pastor Osteen's meetings but had to leave early because she suddenly became short of breath and couldn't breathe."

Almost apologetically he added, "We took her to the hospital only when she turned blue."

After a short pause, I asked, "What are her doctors doing for her?"

His voice revealed a sense of urgency. "They have her in ICU on an intravenous drip and tell us that her lungs are filling up with fluid. They want to perform surgery."

I considered his friend, the girl's father. His eyes cast a blank, forlorn stare at the floor. His hope for her recovery was gradually dissolving. Before I could respond, I was asked, "Can we bring her to your clinic?"

My immediate impulse was to discourage any move away from her current location. She obviously had major heart problems, either congenital or complications of rheumatic fever, possibly even endocarditis. Any discontinuation of her current treatment could result in death. Possibly, her doctors were contemplating valve replacement or other surgery.

Only after I assured them that I would go with them to the hospital the following day were they convinced to keep her in the hospital. Sue had overheard some of our conversation. Her knowing glance in my direction echoed my sentiments exactly.

Eighty thousand jammed Jawaharlal Nehru Stadium that evening. As we approached by car, Dahta slowed to maneuver around the people flooding towards the stadium. In the back seat, Pastor Osteen was visibly moved at the sight. Tears temporarily filled his eyes.

"I am but a messenger boy. I am not the healer. Jesus is the Healer. You do not need to touch me. You need to touch Jesus."

Pastor Osteen was brief and discreet. His obvious intentions were to instruct everyone of his mortality and Jesus' immortality: an attempt to prevent the mass stampede of the previous evening.

"Acts 10 describes Cornelius as a deeply religious man. He prayed daily to God. He attempted to do what was right in God's sight."

The tall speakers at each side of the platform blared his words out over the crowd. I decided to count the people who were sitting cross-legged on the grass in the front row. They were over one hundred feet from the platform, yet I could clearly discern over one hundred twenty individuals in this row alone. There were hundreds of more rows behind.

"Like Cornelius, all of India is deeply religious, seeking God. But you can be very religious and still be lost. You can be religious but still have no peace."

"Jesus told me to go to precious India, go to precious New Delhi. Tell them I will heal them; I will deliver them; I will set them free!"

He spoke many more words about Jesus. He revealed Jesus' concern for each one of them.

Over five thousand stood to accept Jesus. Shortly thereafter, we left to avoid the pandemonium of the night before. Later, however, John called P. G. Vargis who reported many documented miracles. Among these was a woman who had been in a wheelchair for twelve years. She stood up and walked. Another older woman had to walk with a stick. She stood, threw the stick down, and walked. Her husband followed her onto the platform and could do nothing but cry. The parents of a child also could only weep because their son, who had never walked - could only sit - stood and walked. A totally deaf boy began to hear. Many more were healed but time did not allow for their testimonies.

Like Cornelius, India saw the light.

22 OCT

"GOOD NEWS MAHOTSAV. Come and hear the message of peace, love and brotherhood. Main speaker, Dr. John Osteen", declared page eight of The Hindustan Times.

Page one had reported about the increased incidence of HIV cases in Maharashtra districts. Another page described the rampant indebtedness in Western Rajasthan, where cerebral malaria had claimed thousands of lives.

All of India desperately needed the Good News advertised. A message that up until today, had been prohibited from the very newspapers that reported all the bad news.

"The Good News is not that God will forgive man. The Good News is that God has already forgiven man!"

Pastor Osteen had been greeted at Talkadora Auditorium by a hushed audience full of great expectations. As he taught, I could sense a new awakening; a fresh recognition that God quickly forgave even the most vile.

His words were those of a father gently talking to his children.

"Jesus, the Lamb of God, has taken away the sins of the world. Because of that, God has been reconciled to man. Therefore, God is not counting up and holding against man their trespasses. God is not keeping a record of sins. He has cancelled them!"

"If this is so, then why isn't everybody saved?" Pastor Osteen paused, as if expecting an answer from the crowd.

He then answered his own question in this way. "Because many men and women are like a prisoner who refuses to accept a pardon. The courts in the United States have ruled that a pardon is of no effect until it is accepted. Men do not go to hell because of murder, fornication, or other sins. They go to hell because they have not accepted God's pardon; they have not accepted Jesus Christ; they have not accepted Jesus' sacrifice for their sins."

"God has reconciled the world. He has restored India to favor with himself. God has turned His face toward Indians. All we need to do is turn Indians toward God."

The crowd was beginning to stir. Scattered shouts of joy and praise answered each exhortation from the podium. But these were far from disruptive. They only magnified the 'rhema' as it was delivered.

"Get rid of all your religious ideas! Don't worry about the outside: the way they look or the way they are dressed. Don't worry about the way they act. Worry about the spiritual inside, the spiritual condition of Indians."

"Only you are the hope of India!" His emphasis was on the 'you'.

Many had already jumped to their feet. Now others joined in.

"Do you dare tell your nation what you have been told today? Do you dare tell them that God has cancelled their sin? Do you dare tell them that God has restored them to Himself?"

Great jubilation erupted. Everyone was on their feet dancing their praises to the Lord God. The banner behind the stage began to shake. Hindi songs exalted His name like a great heavenly shout.

Dust that had gathered over the years on the red and gold oriental rugs under-foot began to rise. Hundreds of exuberant feet had stirred the Indian soil to new heights. I followed the dust as it ascended towards heaven. My eyes then noticed the banners high near the ceiling.

"REACH THE UNREACHED AND TELL THE UNTOLD."

"KASHMIR TO KANYAKUMAR. INDIA WILL BE SAVED."

"LORD, DO IT AGAIN IN INDIA. LORD, DO IT NOW."

Truly, the Lord was doing it in India. He was doing it now.

Nishi was standing unsteadily in the middle of the room, obviously nervous in her new surroundings. She frequently turned to assure herself that a chair was close, in the event her weak, swollen legs gave way. By the time Sue and I arrived, she was surrounded by her father, her father's friend, Brother Martin, John and Pastor Osteen. Brother Martin was vigorously instructing her in Hindi. Her head was bowed slightly; her eyes almost closed. She had lack-luster black hair which hung limply down her back, with a few isolated strands dangling over her face. Occasionally, her eyelids would slowly open to reveal the fear that resided within.

Pastor Osteen noticed our entrance. He motioned us to his side. As I came near, I realized her identity; the very girl I was to visit in the hospital.

Her father's friend turned to me. With a half smile, he spoke as if apologizing for bringing her here against my advice of the previous day. "Her doctors said she has a hole in her heart and she wasn't getting any better in ICU. It looked to us as if she was getting worse with each passing minute so we decided to bring her here for prayer."

"Did her doctors give you her exact diagnosis?", I asked. He handed me a crumpled piece of paper. I knew that a 'hole in the heart' could be one of several diagnoses, or simply her family's misunderstanding of the doctor's report. (Doctors frequently speak with big words that family members have difficulty comprehending, especially under the duress of a personal medical crisis.)

The paper revealed her diagnosis to be endocarditis, infection of the heart valves, as well as mitral regurgitation and aortic stenosis. The latter two terms indicated malfunctioning valves. As a consequence, she also had pulmonary edema. Essentially her lungs were filling up with fluid which her heart could not properly pump. She had been given claforan and tobramycin, both antibiotics, and several medications to help her heart handle the excess fluid.

I glanced at her again. She was breathing over thirty times per minute with quick, brief inspirations and slow prolonged expirations. She had blue lips and an ashen face. Her heart clearly was losing the battle. Her blue color revealed poorly oxygenated blood due to water-logged lungs. Without the antibiotics and the other medications, I realized she had no chance.

"Sue, lay your hands on her chest as we pray!" Pastor Osteen instructed.

Each of us prayed as the Holy Ghost led. Outside the room, we could hear the muffled clamor of a crowded Talkadora Auditorium just down the hall. All were still praising our Lord Jesus Christ. The morning's message had touched many hearts. Inside the room, we all hoped and prayed that Jesus would also touch poor Nishi's heart.

The prayer was over and Nishi gingerly turned to leave with deliberate steps. Her father's friend turned to each of us and burned his thanks with watery eyes.

As they left, a young man stumbled in. Brother Martin, who was extremely tall and robust, quickly caught him by the shoulders with strong hands. He and the other Indians began to speak in Hindi with this boy, whose emaciated condition exaggerated both his height and prominent cheek bones. A western style dark suit hung loosely off his sharp shoulders.

As they talked with him, he turned his head away, closed his eyes and looked down. Brother Martin and the others suddenly began to speak more intently with him, yet he would not raise his head nor open his closed eyes. His furrowed brow was dripping with beads of sweat.

"What's wrong with him?" John Greiner asked the question that was on all our lips.

Slowly, Brother Martin looked up and said, "He has the AIDS virus." After a short moment of silence he added, "... and he is very much ashamed."

Empathy grew in our hearts. This boy faced only untold pain, misery, and duress. Already he obviously had experienced ridicule, scorn and humiliation. He probably also wondered if God had forsaken him.

"Bless him, Father." Pastor Osteen gently whispered.

Slowly, the boy opened his eyes. The first thing he saw was Pastor Osteen's smile with arms open wide just for him. He took the final step and buried his head into Papa's shoulder.

Later that very same afternoon, Pastor Osteen was invited to the Presidential Palace for a private meeting with India's President. They spoke of Thomas, the doubting apostle who had traveled all the way to India with the Gospel in the first century, fourteen hundred years before the Gospel reached the Americas. The President was presented a Malayalam-English Bible, which he accepted with great gratitude.

Pastor Osteen had been as cordial to Nishi and the boy with AIDS as he was to the President. Jesus had taught that all are welcome at God's table irregardless of their station or 'caste' in society. Not everyone can be a president, but all who declare Jesus Lord, irregardless of their previous sins, is accepted into God's family. God truly is full of mercy, long suffering and slow to anger.

"I have many Hindu friends here in Delhi. I love them and cherish them as such. But I am not shy in telling them that there is just one God, and His name is Jesus!", declared The Most Reverend Alan DeLastro, Catholic Archbishop of New Delhi.

He had just offered the introductory prayer at Jawaharlal Nehru Stadium. Long clerical robes magnified his tall frame, whereas glasses provided an aura of scholarship. But his benevolent demeanor advertized acceptance, despite his official outward appearance. Now he was explaining his ministry and beliefs to Sue and I as we sat next to him on the platform.

He gestured towards the ninety thousand crowding the stadium complex. Occasionally, he would pause to cross a blessing to a follower in the audience.

Referring to those in the crowd, he continued, "Some come from villages where doctors will not go. I don't blame them, of course. Conditions in the villages do not allow for medical practice. No one has the ability to pay."

"Another problem is abortion. Because of the dowry system here, nobody wants girls. So they have begun to utilize technology imported from the west, the ultrasound. If the ultrasound indicates a girl, the poor defenseless thing is aborted and thrown away in the trash."

"So that's why I am so excited about Pastor Osteen's meetings here in Delhi. India needs Jesus! I am glad that we can dissolve doctrinal differences and join you in proclaiming Jesus Christ!"

In the crowd I could see many in wheelchairs, walkers and even crude home-made walking sticks. They were all sitting to the left of the stage. In the midst of them was Joel, who was roaming about with his video equipment. Via his efforts, a pictorial record would be made of not only the crusade, but of the Pastor's Conference as well. He and John had labored tremendously to lug the bulky video equipment through twelve time zones and New Delhi customs. I had to respect his diligence, talents, and even humility. Standing tall in jeans hoisting the heavy camera on his shoulder, he contrasted greatly from the sick and infirm, most of whom were dressed simply and propped up by a relative in some fashion.

Pastor Osteen declared that many were brought to Jesus with all manner of diseases: sick and tormented. "Jesus was moved with compassion as He saw the multitudes. He therefore said, 'Fear not, for I am with you. Be not dismayed, because I am your God. I will help you. I will strengthen you. I will uphold you with the right hand of my righteousness!'"

"Jesus said, 'Come unto Me, and I will answer you!'"

Finally, he said, "Faith is an act: you must act!"

Hunger for God was intense among those in the audience. Many could not wait for Pastor Osteen to complete his sermon and came forward en mass. They acted by faith. Initially, the designated ushers attempted to control the crowd. However, soon it was apparent that many experienced the miraculous move of the Holy Ghost right where they were sitting or standing. Their excitement precipitated others to rush towards the platform.

Among those who related God's power was a nurse. She had been to the crusade two days earlier. During the general prayer, she felt a difference. She therefore was reexamined by her physician who could no longer detect the fibroid tumors. An ultrasound confirmed their absence!

Three young boys had withered, atrophied and useless limbs. They walked for the first time after these legs miraculously straightened!

A man who had been to all the meetings reported total resolution of a congenital cardiac defect. Both his physician and an echocardiogram authenticated his words.

A woman with a painful stiff neck for five years was pain-free.

A man who had been unable to walk for sixteen years, walked.

With tears, another man declared that after attending the past four nights, he finally had peace!

Earlier in the service, John Greiner delivered his testimony and then sang, 'Oh Happy Day'. None of us will ever forget his rendition, obviously inspired by a Force from above. His voice echoed off the concrete pillars and rang through the still night air.

'Happy Day' still rings true in the hearts of Indians. It especially rings in a certain nurse, several boys who can now run and play, a man with a new heart, and another man who no longer hobbles but walks upright.

Like the man with tears, it is a happy day when the tormented finally has peace!

23 OCT

We arrived in the camp by early afternoon. Sue and I unpacked the medications and arranged them on a wooden table just inside the doorway of a centrally located hut. I then began examining the sick under a large tree. The dark, dank rooms afforded by the hut prohibited their use for this purpose. Soon, a large throng of sick Indians gathered around me.

Occasionally, I would stop my examinations long enough to reinstruct the mob around me that I would indeed see everyone, yet only in an orderly fashion. Every time I looked up I would be greeted by pleading eyes and a multitude of patients asking to be next. In Asia, an orderly line is a completely foreign concept. Poverty and lack has taught the concept of 'every man for himself'.

I left my post to see how Sue was faring as she dispensed the medicines. Inside, I found her surrounded by a wall of coughing humanity pushing their prescriptions into her visual space. She was bent over a pile of bags, prescription forms, and assorted pills. Two sisters, as nurses are called in India, were at her side assisting. Immediately, I cleared the room and arranged everyone in a nice neat line.

Within a few minutes this tidy line once again deteriorated into chaos, as did the line around me. Therefore, I began to alternate between examinations and straightening the queues.

Before the afternoon was over, we had examined and treated ninety seven patients, to bring our three day total to two hundred sixty seven. We packed up the remaining medications, which the following day would be given to a good friend and his trusted coworkers. In turn, over the next few months they would take them to the sick in various villages across India, Nepal and Bhutan.

Earlier, Pastor Osteen had exhorted the Christians gathered at Talkadora Auditorium. He warned against discouragement and despair that can sometimes follow great victories. The enthusiasm generated by the current meetings, he knew, could be quenched by the storms of life. He then reminded everyone how he had been coming to India for the past twenty-seven years. His only purpose was to teach the Good News of Jesus Christ. Actions spoke much louder than words. Lakewood Church had made these meetings possible by financing them and even paying up to half the travel costs and all room and board of the attendees.

His words were first met with silence. Spontaneously, song broke out. Gradually, both enthusiasm and intensity of such increased. Many again were dancing in the aisles. They were joyously singing, 'When the Spirit of the Lord comes into my heart I will dance as David danced'. As Pastor Osteen turned to go, the singing ceased and a rhythmic clap erupted, much like that of a ball game. But this was more than a mere athletic contest. It was a celebration of gratitude to one who had brought the words of eternal life. The Spirit of the Lord had come into their hearts.

"Who is this Jesus? Born of the Virgin Mary... baptized by John... healed the sick... set the captives free... nailed to a cross... and rose from the dead."

The public address system broadcast Pastor Osteen's words across the stadium and into the night air. As he spoke, I considered the cricket field as a valley surrounded by the steep mountainous inclines of the stadium. I looked unto the fields of people; many occupied the valley, others engaged the inclines. The fields were genuinely white, ready for harvest.

"Jesus said, 'I am the way, the truth, and the life... I am the resurrection and the life... I am the only way to the Father'."

Repeatedly, the Word was preached boldly with power. Jesus was clearly declared as who He was, and still is; our Savior.

People came running to accept Him. They came with tears and they came with laughter. All were welcome. Brother Martin led them in the sinners prayer. As their hands went up in surrender, they resembled grains of wheat.

The gentle breeze of Jesus was moving them in the night.

Shortly, those who received miraculous healings appeared on the stage. Tonight, we all lingered. We wanted to see this move of the Holy Ghost up close. We saw many withered legs become strong. We witnessed cripples walk for the very first time. Those who had been bound by the devil, were loosed by the Prince of Peace.

In the midst of the crying and laughter, a young Sikh grabbed the microphone. In his other hand were wooden crutches. "I had been crippled from birth!" He brazenly shouted, "tonight, I walked without these crutches for the very first time in my life!"

The drama we beheld was one of great significance. Sikhs are known for their religious fervor. Their religion prohibits them from cutting hair. Their long beards are twisted and drawn up into turbans, a symbol of their piety in a hot, humid Indian climate. To deviate from these traditions would put a Sikh at risk of losing his position in society. Even his family would declare him as if dead. To declare Jesus would be social suicide.

Brother Vargis seized the microphone and asked, "Who did this for you?"

"Jesus did it. He healed me! I now follow only Jesus!"

People began crowding the platform. Again, the scene was similar to that of previous nights. I clutched Sue's hand and fought towards the car. Ultimately, we made it safely. Soon, Joel and Pastor Osteen were also secured inside. Dahta suddenly began to ease away through the crowd. I looked back through the rear window and saw John. His eyes were as big as silver dollars, one arm was trapped by the mob, the other flailing wildly in the air. Obviously, he saw the car move and realized he was about to be abandoned. The consequences of such must have flashed through his mind.

From my position, sheltered in the car, it was quite hilarious. Almost simultaneously, however, we all shouted for Dahta to wait. Once inside, John's heart could be heard beating exuberantly above the noise of the throng around us.

We gingerly made our way through the crowd and onto the city streets. The electricity of the moment gradually faded but the excitement remained. Soon, we were on the road leading to our hotel.

"Well, Doctor, what do you think?"

Momentarily, I would answer Pastor's question. Temporarily, however, I was lost in thought. Over thirty five thousand had accepted Jesus in the five crusade meetings. Countless others would be touched by the combined ministry of the pastors who attended the conference. Contemplating tonight's gathering, I had never seen so many cripples healed in such a short period of time: certainly not in any other Church service; definitely never in any hospital. I had recognized many of the diseases represented. Most were incurable. Many would have spent their lives and possibly livelihood in institutions; even had they been in the America.

A few months later I would read an article written by the noted scientist, Carl Sagan (now deceased). He would conclude that the odds of obtaining a miraculous healing would be similar to winning the lottery. I don't pretend to be an expert on statistics. However, my many years of medical training and medical practice had educated me to the fact that I had obviously just been surrounded by hundreds of lottery winners.

When we had arrived, India was cloaked in darkness. Nothing had changed in years. Plagues were rampant, as were poverty and suffering. Still there remained suffering, misery, distress, and sorrow. But during the last five days, we had all seen the Light overcome darkness.

Then I considered this Jesus. I wondered if even his very own mother, Mary, realized that two thousand years after she witnessed His crucifixion, He would still live to change the hearts and minds of men and women everywhere. I contemplated whether His very own father, Joseph, the carpenter, fathomed that twenty centuries after nails pierced His hands, He would still be the Master Builder of broken hearts and castaway lives.

Indisputably, Jesus can still change the destiny of a nation. More importantly, He has reconciled the sins of the whole world, including India, where the Light is truly overcoming darkness.

"I think, Pastor, "I finally answered, "that we have one great God."

It was a dark, moonless, and steaming filipino night. The unseen waters of the Samar Sea, cloaked in darkness, lapped rhythmically against the also unseen muddy beach. A few hours previously, this beach was bathed with tropical sunlight, revealing our makeshift clinic right in the midst of the fish-market on Zumarraga's waterfront. From the fish-market, a concrete wall sloped down to the sea, which was littered with occasional refuse and a variety of colorful, but faded, fishing boats. The very boat that had labored to bear us across the straits from Catbalogan now lay anchored to the lone pier in the darkness that had swallowed us all. As I scanned the black night, the only lights were those of startling luminous stars overhead, and the dimmer flickers of candlelight and/or kerosene lamps from Daram Island to the west.

Even in the ebony evening, I was hot. My clothes stuck to me like flies to molasses and my sock-less shoes grasped my tired feet like cement. The suffocating heat was tempered only occasionally by a gentle ocean breeze that stirred the coconut palms overhead and the banana trees to my side. It also stirred my anticipation for relief but never seemed to last long enough. I could feel a slight flaming twinge of sunburn radiating from my arms, face and legs. I had forgotten sun-block to protect me from the reflected sunlight off the sea and now my ankles especially felt both the radiant heat and strain of the day.

Fatigue was heavy upon me and the others. We had attended to 204 coughing and sneezing patients in the hot sun already today. I was looking forward to my bucket of well water back at the nipa hut. My turn had not come before it was time for the night meeting, which was just about to commence.

Despite our intentions of providing free medical exams and appropriate medications for the sick, our welcome at noon had been less than cordial. No one appeared at the dock to greet us save several small boys. Their questions yelled to us above the surf were not purposed for answers, but for the laughs and esteem of their peers.

I paused to look at their smirks and devilish glee. Could it be that in them I recognized satan's ridicule?

The Mayor, who never appeared in person, had reportedly suggested the government building near the pier for our clinic. Yet the offer was subsequently rescinded. The next offering was that of the vacant health clinic. But the police chief appeared with bloodshot eyes to re-offer the government building. Again the offer was revoked. Our legs, weary of walking back and forth between the two offerings, decided on the fish market. It was vacant, it was close, and its roof afforded much needed shade. The officials' indecisiveness was thereby abrogated.

I remember wondering whether the local Roman Catholic Priest had anything to do with the decision, or rather, indecision. After all, it was he who had vociferously resisted every other attempt to establish a local Bible-believing Church. He had reportedly incited the populace to persecute the two families of Believers on the island. This persecution took the form of verbal, and sometimes even physical abuse. On at least one occasion, even stoning was threatened to this small, but dedicated band.

Unfortunately, their local Pastor, who was to host us, was gone. He was in Manila. With high hopes, he and his wife had taken their nineteen year old boy, diagnosed with liver cancer (evidently the consequence of chronic active hepatitis B), to the Philippine Government Hospital.

But the boy died. His father and mother had not yet returned.

The generator was now supplying energy for the lights to illuminate the area in front of the government building. Songs of praise to our God began to ring the air via the large speakers we had brought with us. Villagers from the barrio began to gather. Other winds stirred the trees.

Pastor Hercules (Herlie) Montes took the microphone from the other musicians. He was the Pastor of Catbalogan Christian Center. Today he had piloted our boat through the sea. Already tonight he had served as one of the musicians. Now he would be my interpreter. He called my name in the midst of a flurry of Waray. I assumed I was being announced and therefore approached the concrete platform in front of the basketball court that served also as the town's central square. I recalled that a previous attempt to hold a similar evangelistic meeting in this very place ended in a shouting match that the Priest had apparently won. Few had responded favorably.

I surveyed the large crowd that had congregated mostly amongst the shadows by the concrete wall on the opposite side of the court. Somewhere in the darkness, I knew the Priest would be waiting.

18 JUNE

"You will be going to Samar?"

I answered in the affirmative.

"Then we will need to pray especially that the forces of demonic oppression and witchcraft that are prevalent there will not touch you...that the Holy Ghost will preserve you and bring forth victory!"

Pastor Driz' prayer in the car would also prove to be prophetic. He and his driver had just picked us up. But he was not the first to refer to the demonic sorcery of Samar. Earlier, I had spoken at a small but vibrant Church located on Rodriguez Street in the heart of Pasay City. After my words of encouragement, Pastor Jun Mercado had prayed, "...that the strongholds of satan and all witchcraft in Samar be broken..."

Perhaps we were to face divination and sorcery. But with the strong prayers of my filipino brothers and sisters, I was confident in our Delivering God. He would not fail us.

The name of the Church on Rodriguez Street was "Take the Nations for Jesus Church". We expected to do just that in Samar.

Back to the present, I was thankful for the air-conditioning as heat was already rising from the steaming pavement just outside. From my back-seat window I could see the early afternoon wind gently stirring garbage along the gutters. Even on Sunday, Manila's infamous traffic was at its usual standstill. Hawkers of a variety of trinkets and condiments took advantage of the clogged streets by dodging between vehicles, selling their wares. On the curb, crowds had gathered waiting for their desired jeepney or bus. Others, carrying umbrellas to ward off the unrelentless sun and handcloths to sop up inevitable sweat, hurried along the street to limit exposure to the humid air and burning sun to a minimum. Their relief would not be an air conditioned car, office, nor dwelling, but simply a rotating fan, at best, or a sliver of unoccupied shade. Few in the Philippines knew more comforts than these.

Those already in buses, vied for a window seat so that they may hang their head and at least one arm out the window to grasp any bit of available breeze. In this breeze, pollution was heavy with diesel smoke, dust, and grime. Smells of clogged sewers occasionally tempered the usual smell of burnt gasoline and wood smoke. But the nose was not to be insulted alone. Eyes stung with smoke and soot, while ears were met with short beeps, shrill honks, and blaring, muffer-less engines. Away from the traffic, roosters, dogs and humans made sure that eardrums would not lie dormant.

"You know, Dr. Price, when you came last year, not only was my Church strengthened, but even my family was encouraged." Pastor Driz had half turned in his front seat. As we maneuvered through Manila's congested streets, he continued. "My wife had a cyst on her arm. She had been anxious about it since her father previously had cancer. A few days after you prayed for her, and after we read your book, the cyst disappeared, never to return. You, and your book, have been a great blessing to us."

"So I have asked a friend of mine to be at the meetings today. He is a district leader in his denomination, the Christian and Missionary Alliance. Maybe we can arrange some meetings with his Churches for you next time." After a short pause and my expressions of gratitude, he added, "And we need to get you into the mountains of Luzon. There are many tribal areas, especially the Ifugao, that need your medical outreach."

For such, we were headed for his Church in Muntinlupa. All three 70 pound boxes of medications and supplies had cleared customs the day before, making today's clinic possible. Carlos and Hansel were already waiting at the Church. Norma and Roberto had followed us from Manila in their jeepney. Sue, Diane, and I extricated ourselves from the car to face the heat. Before long, Hermie appeared with her niece, a local dentist.

"Father God, we pray that you will be glorified today in this medical outreach...that many will be touched...many be set free...many will come to know you...." We all had gathered near the front of Bible Centered Church. As we held hands in a circle, Pastor Driz' superior, who had made a special trip to be with us, commissioned us all with his prayer.

Everyone took their appointed places. The trickle of patients quickly became a steady stream. Before long, I noticed a common complaint among the children to be unsightly open sores of draining pus and yellow crusts. Some had surrounding cellulitis and edema, others simply festered angrily, devoid of any other appearance of systemic effects. All appeared extremely painful, like burns. Most were located on the scalp or neck. Soon the common denominator became apparent, a history of swimming in the river.

"Give her triple antibiotic ointment and cephalexin." I instructed my interpreter as I turned to the next victim. "...and tell her mother to keep her out of the river." Perhaps, I thought as they turned towards our pharmacy, there would be one less for the polluted Pasig.

The lights had already gone out; the result of yet another brownout. Yet I was on stage, under the only working light, powered via car battery. Of course, also with me, were hundreds of flying insects, attracted by the illuminating rays. With each sentence, I would also taste several bugs. Silently, I prayed for renewed power.

"This is my fourth visit to these islands after my initial trip here seventeen years ago. Others with me tonight are making return visits. We have come back because we love the Philippines. But it is not the islands nor the mountains that we love, although they indeed are beautiful. It is Filipinos that we love. God has brought us back to you...."

I paused to swallow hard. But before I could continue, I could hear a faint, "We love you, too", from somewhere in the back.

Suddenly, all the lights were back on. The rotating fans began to move the air. We praised God in song; we worshiped Jesus by name. A woman sought healing for cancer, another for deliverance from hindering spirits. A young man came for renewed anointing. Some received Jesus for the first time. Others regained fellowship. We were all praying individually, then jointly in one accord.

That day in the clinic, we had seen 220, of which 65 confessed Jesus as Lord. Tonight, more were blessed.

The bugs had dispersed. The light of the World, Jesus Christ, illuminated us.

20 JUNE

"Jesus said, 'In this world you shall have tribulation, but be of good cheer, for I have overcome the world'."

The crowd was scattered across the basketball court. No one stirred. It seemed all were intent, for now, upon my words which Pastor Herlie was translating into Waray. As I spoke, I scanned those in the crowd for the Priest. But the bright lights above me constricted my pupils: recognition of those in the shadows was impossible.

"Tribulation is another word for trouble, or difficulty," I continued. "Today we saw many of you with troubles. Many of you have coughs, pains, weakness, and other sickness. All these are tribulations."

"That is why we came."

Indeed, our travel to this small island in the Visayans had also been full of tribulations. Yesterday, we had met at Manila's domestic airport. It was another hot day and the streets were packed, as usual. The check-in process was not without complications nor oppressive heat as warm bodies vied for a better position in the nonexistent line. A long walk across a blistering tarmac led to the Philippine Airlines Fokker 50 turboprop which was sweltering as it sat idle.

An hour and a half later, we touched down at Calbayog where Rev. Rizzy Montes arranged for our transportation into town. Our small rooms across from the Coconut Planters Land Bank provided both running water and air conditioning. Unfortunately, both were on a temporary and erratic basis. Through the night, each motion on our bed was accompanied by a loud crunch of the plastic-covered mattress. But I was thankful for the constant drone of the window unit which drowned-out the ubiquitous roosters who knew not night from day.

The Bong na Bong bus departed the marketplace at 6:30 AM. I was crammed into a seat designed for two Filipinos, with my long American legs draped over the engine housing. Sue was in the seat behind me with Joey Montes, Rizzy's daughter who would prove to be invaluable in the days ahead.

There were numerous stops, both scheduled and unscheduled to pick up passengers along the roadside. A sharp rap to the side of the bus would be the signal for the driver to stop. Two quick knocks indicated all was clear for the driver to resume. In this manner, we traveled south, first along the coast, then through mountain passes, and finally down to the sea once again as we approached Catbalogan from the northwest. Close to Catbalogan, the coastline became familiar as I recognized barrios I had visited seventeen years previously. The azure sea was as calm as I remembered it, with colorful fishing boats scattered across the horizon. Coconut palms gracefully rose from the shores.

After a breakfast of rice, pineapple juice, and lukewarm beef (I think) stew at the Family Place Restaurant, we headed towards the market where provisions for our stay on Zumarraga Island would be gathered. Amongst much bustle and gesticulation on the part of the sellers, we viewed the fresh catch of the night before. Catfish squirmed in small vats next to ink-covered squid and octopus. Muscles and shrimp were carefully arranged for best exposure, of which the ubiquitous flies took great advantage. The smells of the sea and sewage suddenly struck me in the face as I turned to see Sue motion me toward daylight.

Once out from under the canopy of the market, I heard the squeals. Carlos led me to the pigs, most with legs bound tightly. Occasionally, one of the victims would vigorously grunt and struggle against the ropes. They all seemed to fully understand the seriousness of their situation and the consequences that were to soon befall them. Down the street, the consequences were clearly visible as men hacked away at dismembering the legs from an undignified bacon carcass. A few feet away boys hung the butchered legs from a hook, while women cleaned intestines on a flat and greasy wooden table. Flies buzzed happily about. I followed one of the cardinal rules of infectious disease prevention by keeping my mouth shut.

Back at our jeepney, the rice had been loaded as well as enormous bunches of flat, stubby bananas. The last to come would be the bottled water. A rain shower turned into steam as it hit the street before we were fully loaded. Once the shopping was complete, we headed towards the pier and our awaiting fishing boat.

One by one, we boarded...via a board. A single plank bridged the gap between the concrete pier and the boat. Balancing was assisted via a bamboo handrail held across the chasm by two men.

Once all supplies, baggage, and people were aboard, we pushed off only to be caught in a neighboring boat's net. Additional maneuvers brought us back to the pier and then suddenly upon the stern of another boat. Utilization of bamboo poles freed us from both boats and concrete and within the hour we began to gain speed as we eased away from the coast. Behind us were the grey warehouses and tall red Philippine Long Distance Telephone (PLDT) tower of the Catbalogan waterfront. Before us was the calm Samar Sea and the islands of Daram, Parasan, and Zumarraga. To our left, the east, was Maqueda Bay.

Before long we had put several miles of sea between us and Samar. The tall PLDT tower was but a miniature on the horizon when the engine first died.

For a few minutes, we drifted aimlessly as several Filipinos descended into the bowels of the boat to correct the problem. Soon, the engine came to life again, only to die quickly. A longer wait resulted. Off to our right, rain clouds pelted the sea and hid Samar from view. All around us were islands. I counted fourteen. Unfortunately, all were miles away. Closer to us were many fishing boats, most much smaller than ours.

With time the engine came back to life and once again we were on our way. Just as we were to make a wide turn towards Zumarraga, the motor quit once more. The rainclouds were now behind us but rapidly approaching. We were sure to get wet. I was simply hoping it would be the rain, and not the seawater seeping through the stern and bow.

We all silently considered the troubles we had endured. It was as if someone was doing everything to prevent our disembarkation on Zumarraga. As the rain hit us, the motor caught life and propelled us forward.

As we made our final approach, I stood on the bow. I remember thinking, "Despite your petty tribulations, devil, we're here. God has delivered us to victory."

Our reception was cool, as stated previously. Soon, however, we set up clinic in the vacant fishmarket. Like Peter and Andrew, we, too, hoped to catch men that day.

Back to the present, I knew the tribulations we faced in coming paled to those faced daily here in Zumarraga. Today I had seen tumors, open sores, and bodies racked with arthritis. Many constantly coughed, sneezed, and attempted to clear clogged bronchi. This was but the tip of the iceberg as many suffered for years without the benefit of even a simple tylenol while living on an island without running water, air conditioning, electricity, or ice.

But their worst tribulation and fear was that they also faced darkness alone without God. They had no peace. They knew there was a heaven but weren't quite sure how to get there.

Tonight it would be their time to be sure.

"We examined many of you today because you had tribulations of sickness. We then gave you medications. Both the exam and the medicines were free."

I paused temporarily, and then continued. "But we also came to tell you of a far greater free gift. It is a gift that is much more valuable than medicines or medical exams. All you have to do, just like the medicines today, is to take it."

Herlie translated as I expounded about Jesus, God and the devil. I explained how Jesus was born, and how He lived going around doing good. Then I revealed how He died, taking our place and thereby overcoming the devil in our behalf.

"God has sent us to you tonight to let you know that He is not angry with you for your mistakes. He is not sending judgment upon you. He simply wants you to accept the free gift of eternal and abundant life. He wants you to know that Jesus has truly overcome the world for you."

No one stirred. All remained attentive. The priest, if he were here, had not yet revealed himself. Only the Holy Ghost was moving upon hearts.

Then I told them how Jesus healed me of an incurable illness. After I disclosed these details, I concluded by saying, "Just as sure as I know He healed me, I am sure that by accepting Jesus, you can be assured of going to heaven."

The first one down to accept Jesus as Lord, was a man in a green shirt. After he came, it was as if the entire crowd came. Sixty came that night. Earlier during the clinic, 175 accepted Jesus.

The significance of the man in the green shirt had not yet dawned upon me.

21 JUNE

Roberto said that the roosters work in shifts. It was just that the night shift worked so noisily.

Before going to sleep, I had opened the wooden shutters of the nipa hut to allow any breeze to enter. As I did, both Sue and I noticed the roaches on the curtain. I followed the curtain down from the window and saw that it draped over the mattress on which we were sleeping.

"What do you want me to do with it?" I was referring to the remaining roach."

"Nothing." She answered with tired resignation.

"OK. But remember to sleep with your mouth closed."

But the creatures of the night were not limited to roosters and roaches. Later, some local filipinos, in order to show their appreciation, serenaded us below our window. Sue and I slept through the entire hour of singing. The others, sleeping on the floor, enjoyed (albeit reluctantly) the entire performance.

By 9:00 AM, we had set up clinic once more in the fishmarket. Christian workers from Samar registered the patients. They were then directed towards one of the three physicians located on one side of the permanent concrete tables where fish were sold on market days. On the other side of these was the lone dentist, busy extracting one tooth after another. Dr. Isidro Astorda heard of our clinic and quickly volunteered to attend to the dental needs. We provided the supplies, donated by several dentists in Houston. He supplied the muscle. Between my assigned patients, I could see that he had gathered quite a crowd. Not only could dentists relieve much suffering, they also provided a much more exciting show than all of the medical doctors combined.

Tess was with us once again. Only a few weeks previously she had been house-confined due to varicella. She had obviously contracted this severe case of chicken pox from one of her pediatric patients in Manila. Nevertheless, despite the heat and inconvenience, she was vigorously examining the children.

From the doctors and dentist, all were directed towards Carlos and Diane. They sweated near the water's edge recording names and diagnoses with respective treatment. Then Sue, Norma, and Roberto counted out the appropriate medications while Hermie and Hansel explained the respective directions. Finally, Christians from Samar explained the Gospel message to each and prayed for all. The opportunity to accept Jesus occurred at that time, after receipt of free exams and medications.

Towards the end of the morning, just after the lukewarm coca-cola arrived, I noticed a young woman sitting nearby staring daggers my way. She had done the same the day before. Norma, Hermie, and Hansel noticed her as well. Soon, Diane had joined them in counseling and praying for her. Deliverance from depression and bad memories was hers that day via the blood of Jesus!

By 3:00 PM we were all on the dock. The warm breeze off the blue sea was a welcome relief to the still, sweltering air inland. Our bags and supplies had been loaded aboard the fishing boat. Now it was our turn to board, once again,... via the board.

As we turned towards the island, we noticed him for a final time. He wore his usual smile and long, unkempt, stringy hair. He had loitered about the two days of clinics and had been at the night meeting. It was then, just after we began praying for those who came for prayer, that he first approached me.

"Where's Sheila?" he asked.

I looked at him and then behind me. I wasn't sure it was I that he was addressing. But it was obvious to me by his slurred speech, bloodshot eyes, and fruity breath that he had been drinking something stronger than coca-cola.

"Where's Sheila?" He asked me again.

"Who's Sheila?" I finally responded.

His eyes widened and with an intonation of surprise he asked, "You mean you're divorced?" Abruptly as he came, before I could deny his charges and set him straight, he left.

A few minutes later I saw him approach Sue. From where I stood, I couldn't hear the conversation but I could read her lips as she told him her name. Immediately, he came to me and said with an air of authority, "Her name's Sue!"

Now he was waving to us as we backed away from the pier.

"What a shame." Sue said.

"What do you mean?" I asked.

"What else does he have? On this island, what is there to do but get drunk? There is nothing for him here, and up until now, little chance of hearing about Jesus and the Gospel message. He has little chance of changing his station in life. He has little hope."

After a pause, while we all waved to him, she continued, "Without Jesus, what is there to look forward to but misery and boredom. We must pray that the local Church will reach him, and those like him, with the Gospel."

Even before he was out of sight, and just a few hundred feet from shore, the motor died. After several minutes, we were on our way again. Before the second, more prolonged delay that left us in the middle of the Samar Sea, miles from land, Rev. Rizzy's son commented, "That was such a great word you gave last night. So simple and easy to understand."

We were sitting near the bow. I was attempting to maneuver myself so that I was out of the direct sunlight. The drift of the boat was gradually readjusting the shaded areas.

"Thank you." I responded with a smile. "That's the way I think, simple-minded."

"The response was more than we expected," he continued. "Even the Roman Catholic Priest was saved."

Suddenly, my attention was off the shade and on to what he had just divulged. "What did you say?"

"That was a good word you gave."

"No. I mean about the Priest."

"The Priest accepted Jesus," he answered nonchalantly.

I suppose my look of surprise prompted him to reveal more details. "He was the one who came forward first last night...the one in the green shirt. If you remember, only after he came did the others come."

I turned to Sue and Norma who were both sitting close by. "Did you hear? He said that the Priest got saved!"

The news spread like wildfire amongst our group. Of course, to the locals, this was old news. But they also began to show their excitement after a bit more prodding.

Up until now, the two Christian families had been meeting in one of the homes. In the past two days, 394 accepted Christ, including the local Priest who had formerly opposed them! They would need a better place to meet. While on the island, they had shown us the land that they had already purchased for a building.

I turned to Norma once again. "Tell me again how much it would cost to build a Church?"

"They said just two thousand dollars."

Back on Zumarraga, the alcoholic with the unkempt hair had likely gone back to his hut; and maybe to his bottle.

22 JUNE

"For you." I handed a signed copy of my book to Joey at mid-morning. It was the usual time for the filipino morning merienda. But we were busy seeing hundreds of patients. The local authorities had graciously allowed us use of the clinic just off Pier 1 in Catbalogan. The waiting areas were crowded with the sick. Joey had coordinated all aspects of our visit. I wanted her to know that she was appreciated.

Later I would learn that she had left a good job to return to help her parents in their outreach to Samar and surrounding islands. They had over 80 churches spread across the region. Tomorrow, she would show us the islands of Santo Nino, Camandog, and Almagro. From the black sand beach where we stood, they looked so serene. But I knew they were every bit as needy as Zumarraga which we had seen up close.

"Thank you so much," she said in accepting the gift.

I know she appreciated the gesture. I hope the 564 patients we saw that day also appreciated our effort: even if to some, it would not correct all their ills.

"Don't be afraid, only believe. These were the words used by Jesus to a man whose daughter was dying. He was saying, don't be afraid, God will find a way."

Night had fallen and Catbalogan Plaza was cloaked in darkness, save the few lights near the stage. Lower wattage lights lined the surrounding street and houses. The tall PLDT tower rose above to my right with slowly blinking red beacons. The street was occupied by passing pedicabs, some with headlights, most of which barely penetrated a few feet ahead. The majority of pedicabs, however, had no light source. Other than these, the square was in murky shadows. Even the statue of the revered Jose Rizal at the very forefront of the square, was in darkness.

I was speaking to the crowd made up of local residents and those passing by. Children were frolicking off to the side of the square. Others milled about Rizal's statue. With the microphone, however, even those sitting in their homes across the street could hear me.

Again, Pastor Herlie was my interpreter. His Waray echoed down the street.

Before I began speaking, the musicians had sung about God finding a way. As I listened to them, the Holy Ghost gave me the message I was to speak.

I talked of faith, fear, and the author of each. "...God has not given us a spirit of fear, but of power, love, and a sound mind. Choose faith, don't live in fear...."

Midway through, a mange-covered dog jumped up on stage and sauntered across it to stop just in front of me. Throughout the rest of my time, he would repeatedly get up and down, walking back and forth. Since everyone else ignored him, so did I. But this total irreverence did not prevent God from moving upon lives.

"Turn away from the devil and his fear. Turn to God. Faith in Him will help you fight the battles of this life. And like the man with Jesus whose daughter was delivered back to him both alive and healed, God will find a way for you, too."

Tears flowed as we all prayed for those who came forward. The dog was gone, but God was present.

We had seen 1213 patients in four days of clinics. Of these, 769 gave their hearts to Jesus. We had gone to a remote region of the earth, yet God was there. We had seen Him move upon the people. He changed their lives in a nuclear instant.

Overhead, the red beacons continued to slowly flash on and off relentlessly atop the PLDT tower. From that tower, communications were sent all across these islands, of which there were over 7000. Looking at the tears, and thinking about those on the islands that have not yet heard about the true, unadulterated Gospel, I prayed out silently to God, "Oh, but for more lives, more lives to go where no one wants to go."

I thought of the lives with me. Carlos and Hansel had taken vacation time to serve Sue and I, making sure our needs were met and doing whatever we asked. They even provided additional snacks and nourishment along the way. I also thought of Diane who had scarcely traveled outside of the USA prior to this trip. Yet she had traveled alone across the Pacific and had endured nights without running water and electricity on the floor of a bamboo hut. Hermie also had taken vacation time to help. She had prayed and sweated under less than optimal conditions, surrounded by hoards of coughing and sneezing patients. Tess also sacrificed time away from her duties in Manila. Even shortly after being very sick herself. Roberto and Norma were always there to do all I asked, sometimes even before I thought of it. Their only purpose was for filipinos to hear the Gospel, irregardless of who received the credit. Sue had endured the heat, inconvenience, roaches, and deprivations to count out medicines. The accommodations were less than five star on the day we reached Zumarraga, which was also our fourteenth wedding anniversary.

Joey and the other local filipinos endured far worse than we, yet did all to accommodate us. What we called tribulations during our travel are what they call daily life. Finally, I remembered Pastor Suarez, the Pastor on Zumarraga. He had lost his nineteen year old son. I would also learn later that he had lost a teenage daughter as well just a few years previously. His cost to spread the Gospel was high. But he was coming back to an island changed by God.

The PLDT has the ability to enter into every island and every barrio. With lives such as these, I expect God to enter every island, every barrio, and every life. Then there will be more tears: tears of joy.

I am confident that God will find a way.

BRAZIL JULY 1995

Rio De Janeiro

28 JULY

His message had been videotaped earlier and was currently being delivered via monitors located on each side of the platform. The acoustics echoed his Portuguese off the convention hall walls. He was deliberate. Even I, without the benefit of the translation, could detect his earnestness. He obviously had an important point for his Brazilian audience.

His listeners had gathered in Rio De Janeiro. They were ADHONEP, an association of Christian businessmen. Others had come as well. All 4000 plus were held by his words.

He had not attended in person because such was impossible. He was speaking from his prison cell.

His incarceration was the result of his actions. His actions had resulted in his freedom. His freedom was the crux of his message. But he remained behind bars.

Fernando Carvelho sat beside us on the platform. Ralph Littlejohn was at my side as we heard the translation.

"He had heard about the fire", Fernando whispered.

"What fire?" I asked.

Ralph answered, "One of Custodio's factories was burning. He immediately came out while the fire raged. It appeared all would be lost. But Custodio prayed and with the wave of his hand, the wind suddenly changed direction and the fire was extinguished!"

"That's correct," Fernando agreed. "The fire was such big news, or rather, the putting out of the fire was such news, that many of the major newspapers here in Brazil reported it. And that is where this convicted felon heard about Custodio."

I had heard about him as well from Ralph. Custodio Pirez was the business-man that led ADHONEP. He had relinquished his many business responsi-bilities to his sons so that he could devote 100% of his time to the work of God in Brazil and other latin countries. I had met him for the first time earlier in the day.

The convict's testimony proceeded. Another sound could not be heard, save the whispered translation provided by Fernando. "So it was at the time when many criminals here in Brazil would kidnap the wealthy and offer them for ransom. This man is saying that he decided to kidnap Custodio for this very purpose. So he went to a witch and asked her opinion regarding his plan."

Macumba, I knew, was a mix of spiritism imported from Africa with the slave trade. Years ago, as Portugal was colonizing South America, wealthy land-owners imported Africans to work their fields. These slaves quietly continued their umbanda rites even though their owners had forcibly converted them to Catholicism. They simply substituted every Catholic saint with a pagan coun-terpart. To this day, candles on the beach or remnants of chicken sacrifice in a deserted lot indicate that macumba and its witches are very much a part of Brazilian life. I would later ask our driver about these sacrifices. His reply was that the chickens were the only ones we know about. "We don't know," he had said, "About the other sacrifices made behind closed doors." Even the most sophisticated of Brazilians has a figa, a charm in the form of a fist with the thumb thrust between second and third fingers. It is supposed to ward off the evil eye and provide luck. A recent president of Brazil actually held se-ances in the presidential palace every Friday with the help of a witch from Salvador. (Of course, he was driven from power: so much for the protecting power of his gods.)

"But," Fernando continued, "he says that the witch told him to stay away from Custodio. She told him that this man has more power than even she and any attempt upon him will surely fail. But, he said, he disregarded the witch and proceeded with his plan."

I turned once again to inspect this man. Custodio was standing off to my left with his hands lifted in praise to Jesus. He wore glasses and had a slightly receding hairline. He wasn't a big man, perhaps even slight in physical stature. But his Jesus had made him mighty.

Suddenly, the crowd erupted in applause. We turned to Fernando. He relayed the message with unchecked excitement. His whisper had given way to an almost shouting tone to be heard above the accolades of the crowd. "He said that as he and his accomplices attempted to abduct Custodio, all four of their tires blew out. Of course, their attempt was a failure. They were apprehended and convicted."

"Once in jail, he had contemplated the recent course of events. The witch had indicated that Custodio had more power than she. Truly, four tires blowing out demonstrated this fact. He, too, wanted this power. He sent a message to Custodio."

"Custodio came to the prison. The man asked for forgiveness, which, of course, Custodio granted. But he also received forgiveness for all his sins. Jesus had entered into his heart."

"Now," he says, "even though he remains in prison, he is finally free."

29 JULY

He said that he has the same disease that you spoke of and wants prayer."

I looked at the Brazilian that Fernando spoke of. His wife stood close to his side to help support him. His face was etched with pain. I remembered the pain. My heart went out to him.

I took him by the hand and as I looked into his eyes full of tears I prayed that in the Name of Jesus he be healed, reminding all that we prayed according to God's Word, "...that where two or three are gathered in His Name, there He is, and whatever we ask in the name of Jesus, He will accomplish...."

The prayer was soon over. "Obrigado." His wife had spoken thanks for both of them. As they slowly walked away, I knew that they faced battles. But I was sure they would also receive all God promised if they endured to the end.

"He wants prayer for his nephew. He has AIDS." With Fernando's words I turned to face another. He handed me a small piece of paper with his nephew's name. The AIDS epidemic had hit Brazil with a vengeance. Lifestyles had made sure that few families would be spared its effects. I prayed and we believed for him, knowing that there is no distance in prayer: also recognizing that God truly was his only hope.

I had just spoken in front of over 3000 who had attended the morning session of ADHONEP. Since another speaker was to follow me, no altar call was given. Yet as we exited the stage from the back, those in need came around the partitions to find us. There in the darkness away from the lights, we prayed. God heard us even in the darkness.

Ralph took me by the arm, "Let's go Dr. Price. The car is waiting." But before we made it to the car that was already nearby, another approached speaking Portuguese. He told us of his boat ministry on the Amazon based near the equatorial city of Manaus. He proceeded to invite us to join them at some future time ministering to the medical and spiritual needs of the destitute along the riverbanks.

Finally, we were back in the car, en route to our hotel. Ralph turned to me. "I bet if you had given an altar call, thousands would have responded. I could see how they followed your every word. It's the Holy Ghost!"

It was the Holy Ghost that also led Custodio Pires to establish the fellowship of businessmen back in 1982. Ralph had responded to his letters and had come to counsel him regarding his dream. Over the years, Ralph had returned many times and had traveled throughout the region with him.

I thought of what these two had accomplished over the years. Through Christ, they had done valiantly. Then I considered my next audience immediately after lunch; the youth meeting. It would be my job, I decided, to encourage them to do likewise.

"The people that do know their God shall be strong and do mighty exploits!" I began. "All of us who are young, especially when we first get saved, want to do great and mighty things for Christ: we want to make a difference for God in this evil day." I then related how that was my dream, and how God led me to become a physician.

"But, the devil did all he could to discourage me. I made mistakes like everyone. And then I was afflicted with an incurable degenerated hip. There appeared to be no way for me to walk out my front door pain free, much less all over the world to declare the works of the Lord."

As I waited for my Portuguese interpreter to complete his translation, I viewed the crowd. Before I began, they had been a boisterous multitude of about 1800, with seemingly unchecked energy. Yet, they were faced also, like me, with severe attacks by the enemy. He was doing all he could to bring them down and keep them from reaching God's potential. Some likely were not saved. Friends and family had brought them. So far they appeared to enjoy the singing. Now it was time for them to face the reality of life: the reality of Jesus Christ.

"But today I am doing just that," I continued, "walking pain free all over the world to tell about Jesus. Whereas before I could scarcely walk a few steps out my front door, now I am able to trek even steep mountain trails."

"Jesus Christ healed me."

"You, too, can reach your potential and do mighty exploits. You, too, can be strong for Jesus."

"But how?" I asked them. And then I immediately answered, "By simply knowing your God. By knowing your God you can be the masters of your own destiny."

I then reminded them of their God: of how Jesus was in heaven interceding to the Father just for them; how God the Father was slow to anger and full of compassion.

"...with Christ, you can be directed towards heaven, have deliverance from demonic powers, and possess dominion in this life like kings and queens; children of the Most High God!"

I gave an invitation. All save two to three hundred came forward. We prayed and interceded for them. The Holy Ghost seared their desires for eternity.

As I saw their tears, something told me that these are the strong men and women that will do mighty exploits to change Brazil.

30 JULY

Christ the Redeemer towered 98 feet above us as we stood at its stone base. In the middle of the concrete chest was a heart, signifying the sacred heart of Christ. Truly, God's heart beats for all those in this city of millions and this country of multimillions.

We were atop Mount Corcovado. Through the haze of the afternoon, we could see to the east Pao de Acucar, Sugar Loaf. Its black volcanic rock contrasted with the blue waters of the surrounding Guanabara Bay and lush green foliage at its summit and base. The enormity of this bay with its many islands led the Portuguese explorer, Goncalo Coelho, to mistakenly assume this body was the mouth of a river. He therefore named it Rio De Janeiro, since the date of his discovery was January 1, 1502.

To the southwest, between other towering mounts of volcanic rock, we could see the old National Hotel, the location of the first ADHONEP convention back in 1982. Ralph had told me some meetings had lasted into the wee hours of the morning. God had truly jump-started this movement during those early hours so many years ago.

Next to this now closed hotel, was the Intercontinental Hotel, Rio. Earlier in the day we had sat with Custodio, his daughter Rozane, and other members of his family. Via Rozane's English, we received and gave thanks to Custodio for the opportunities here in Brazil. Through his efforts, I was able to share about Christ's love and healing power, not only via my presentations of the day before, but also through the Portuguese translation of my book. He had also apologized for his inability to arrange for a medical outreach among the favelas, the slums, which we had wanted to conduct. "...too much governmental red tape....", he had said. But he assured that it could be corrected for the next time, not only here in Rio, but in other locations across Brazil, even in Amazonia among the Indian villages.

It was in the Intercontinental that Ralph had showed me one more aspect of their handiwork. "I had shown Custodio one of our American coins, which was inscribed with, 'In God We Trust'. He got so excited about it that he used his influence in the government to have this done on every Real note."

With that he took a purple and blue five Real note and handed it to the attendant behind the desk in the hotel lobby. "What does that say?" he asked him.

"Deus seja louvado," he responded.

"No, I mean in English," Ralph exhorted.

"It means, 'to God be glory'."

From Corcovado the favelas could be seen in almost every direction. They hugged the mountainsides and most hillsides that are deemed unsuitable by the more economically well-off. Their brick, mortar, tin and plywood structures look as uninhabitable as they are precarious hanging over steep precipices. We had driven through some of the safer ones to see their inhabitants up close. We received many blank stares common to those with little hope. We had also seen some of the outward effects of poverty: barefoot children with open purulent sores as well as bloated bellies and few clothes. Their families had flocked to Rio from northeast Brazil in hopes of economic relief, only to find life more difficult in a perilous, and hazardous favela.

To the southeast and south were the famous Copacabana and Ipanema beaches. Although golden sands lined with fine hotels and elegant condominiums gave every appearance of opulence, few visitors to such evade the traps of the gangs of homeless children that steel and rob to survive. Some are orphans. Others simply had been abandoned by their families due to financial difficulty. These are the families that cannot even afford the rent in the favelas. Rather, they live in rickety shacks alongside highways and under viaducts. But these shacks do not provide sufficient room for the many children. Thus the youngsters are abandoned. The resulting adolescent gangs are forced to make their own way. But not only do they face life's cruel problems without fathers and mothers to guide and protect them, they have also become the targets of paid death squads. On July 23, 1993, 70 were murdered as they slept on the steps of the downtown Candalaria Church by a group of hooded men. Five police officers still await trial for their alleged part in this infamous act. For the unwanted castaways, even the steps of a church harbor no security.

Finally, many prostitutes ply their trade along these very same 'chic' beaches. Their modus operandi seems to spread to most other residents, especially during Carnival. This is the five days prior to lent when seemingly the entire town and multitudes of tourist join in a frenzy of debauchery and illicit acts; a modern day Sodom and Gomorrah.

Christ the Redeemer, the statue atop Corcovado, has outstretched arms. But no statue, designed by human hands, can clearly demonstrate the availability of Jesus Christ's open-armed love to all: even for the slum-dweller, the sophisticate, the prostitute, the widow, and the unwanted orphan.

Later, as dusk approached, Ralph and I headed for Aeroporto do Galeao. We arrived safely at the United Airlines ticketing desk. An agent took my ticket and began his usual security questions.

But Ralph interrupted him.

"Do you know Jesus?" he asked.

The young man's response was one of astonishment. Obviously, few tourists have Christ on their minds. Before he could regain his composure, Ralph said, "Let's make sure!" He proceeded to lead him in the sinner's prayer. Obediently, the young man repeated Ralph's every word.

After the last "amen" and a pat on the back, Ralph hurried off to confirm his seat on Varig. The agent completed my required security check. Once completed, he politely advised me to proceed for ticketing located behind him. As I proceeded, he stopped me.

"And sir," he added, "thank you for telling me about Jesus."

In his eyes, I could see the tears. They were the tears of a thankful heart: the tears that I wish for all Brazilians.

UKRAINE – JUNE 1996

3 JUNE

Our final approach brought us low over the Black Sea Coast. Landfall revealed row after row of tombstone slabs surrounded by rectangles of brown earth, the trails of yesterday's vehicles. But today there were no vehicles. There was only a shadow of human existence in the midday sun.

Next were the bare fields, followed by the apartment buildings. Like the cemetery plots, they were uniformly dull: ashen gray, and old. Tall poplar trees formed uniform borders. Occasional playground equipment bronzed in the sun on asphalt bases. Still, there was no sign of life.

Our altitude regressed allowing poplar, locust, and birch trees obscure from view the apartment buildings. The cracked runway greeted Lufthansa flight 3246 in a not too unfriendly way. We slowed at the far end of the runway and turned towards the terminal. Our turn brought the helicopters, parked in tall grass just off the tarmac, into clear view. Neglect had faded the blue "AEROFLOT" on their fuselage. Blades were missing. Tires had been pirated. Doors were either absent or left ajar. Closer to the terminal, large biplanes of similar disrepair, markings, and airworthiness served as a sad but clear commentary on the world's largest airline. Not a living soul was in sight. I had flown over the cemeteries. Now, for all appearances, I was in one.

Playgrounds were vacant. Pirated aircraft lay disabled. Apartment buildings seemed abandoned. Grass everywhere was unkempt, growing wildly. From every appearance, the population had fled, looting all items of value. Or perhaps, the land lay quarantined.

But the Ukrainians had not fled. They existed, but only in the shadows. Their phantom existence was not new, but a way of life.

Over the centuries, Ukraine has endured insult and indignity. Ghengis Kahn's

153

grandson was one of the first to pillage as his Mongol army shattered the ninth century Ukrainian empire. For those who survived, life was demanding and cruel on the cold Ukrainian steppes. They soon fell victim to the expansionist dreams of a unified Polish-Lithuanian state. The Ukraine, meaning "borderland", soon became a refuge of runaway criminals, slaves and others who fled tyranny of nearby kingdoms and states. Their lives were far from tranquil as the Cossacks, as this amalgamation of peoples came to be known, were at constant war with one foreign ruler after another. In 1654, they finally thought they had attained peace by accepting protection from the northern Russian Empire. But they would soon find that protection came at great sacrifice. The Czars expanded serfdom into their protectorate, and systemized slavery became well entrenched while landowners with connections prospered. The Holy Russian Empire's alliances delivered World War, which in turn, brought typhus and death. Then Czar Nicholas II abdicated power to the Bolsheviks. For a short period, Ukraine stood alone as an independent nation until Lenin's Bolsheviks "liberated" Ukraine, incorporating the land into a new soviet socialist republic. A more miserable life could not have been imagined yet became reality when Stalin manufactured famine to eradicate the landowners. Consequently, as Stalin was maneuvering his political machine into absolute power, seven million Cossacks starved in the very breadbasket of the U.S.S.R. Those who protested were massively deported to Siberia and Central Asia where many more died. The new landlord, the State, extorted even greater sacrifice on the proletariat it was created to serve. A series of five year plans accomplished little except additional exiles, pogroms, and shortages. Working cadres and their families were no more than sacrificial lambs for the well being of card-carrying communists and the State. Yet the State did little to protect the workers from the ravages of World War II as another six million died. Finally came Chernobyl, a category seven nuclear accident that still eats away at lives and hinders every attempt for new Ukraine to attain economic freedom.

Concurrently, disease has badgered Ukrainian life over the centuries. Great fevers that had gone by the names of Typhoid, Crimean Hemorrhagic, Relapsing, and Trench had joined with Cholera, Typhus, Tuberculosis, Pneumococcus, and Hemophilus to remain untrained by the lime, formalin, and white quarantine crosses of the early 1900's. Today, these have not disappeared. Cholera killed again last year. Diphtheria had been killing and maiming for several years. Now, organized crime has taken advantage of new freedoms to provide illicit drugs and a 51% AIDS rate among their customers. Chernobyl may simply symbolically represent an erodible infrastructure: not even a sarcophagus can hide death's quarantine on the land.

UKRAINE – JUNE 1996

I gazed again upon decrepit planes and helicopters as I pondered Ukraine's tribulations. Despite every demonic force unleashed here, Ukraine had eked out an existence. God had not allowed total annihilation. He had people here who, despite all odds, had held onto His Word. They had humbled themselves, they had prayed, and they had sought His face despite insurmountable odds. He, in turn, had heard from Heaven, He had forgiven their sin, and He was healing their land.

The plane had rolled to a stop. At the foot of the stairs leading to the tarmac, I finally experienced Ukrainian life. "Passport!" she barked in soviet monotone. I produced it and she waved me on. My transport was the waiting trailer bus. An old orange truck would pull us to the terminal.

"ODESSA" was in large block letters in both cyrillic and roman script. A hammer and sickle, the old soviet logo, separated the two on the terminal's face. I shuffled with the other passengers through the only open door. A spartan entry hall welcomed us. Exposed wires hung haphazardly from the ceiling. In one corner, these lines had blackened and cracked the plaster. The line of passengers led directly underneath the toasted plaster to another room. Acid smoke, and acrid body odor choked me once inside this dark hallway. We were waiting one by one to be attended by immigration officers within plywood booths. I soon realized that they worked without a sense of urgency. My jet lag only slowed the time.

"I have these papers from immigration...," I began but was stopped short by a wave of the officer. I was now directly in front of a burly customs official. I had brought with me ten bulging boxes of medical supplies. With these, I hoped to ease a little of the suffering that I had heard so much about over the past few years. I had been advised just days earlier that all I needed to clear these supplies through customs was to present the documents I had received via fax. They had supposedly been prepared in Russian by the customs department in Nikolaev to allow the free importation of medical supplies. I had stood at the end of the line which allowed me to view passengers going before me. Many were searched, some more vigorously than others. But I knew that such would not be my fate because of the documents in my pocket. Self assuredly, I presented these to the officer.

As he reviewed them, I knew it would be just a matter of seconds before he would wave me through. In fact, I thought he may even command a few of his men to assist me with the load. After all, these papers had been prepared by the Ministry of Health and would reveal that humanitarian aid would be delivered free to the sick. I waited patiently, content that soon I would be on my way.

"Gavarite Parusski?" he asked. I remembered only a little of my college Russian that I had studied over twenty years ago. But I knew enough to say I needed an interpreter. "Fat chance," his eyes told me.

Soon he had a superior with him. She knew only a little more English than he.

"You must leave boxes, go to customs house at port for signature authorizing release of boxes," she haltingly but authoritatively declared. By that time I had reinforcements in the form of Bob Greiner who had driven with Serge Vivtuik and an English interpreter from Nikolaev. They had been allowed into the customs area a few moments earlier at the guard's insistence to help me understand him. Unfortunately, Dr. Peter, the deputy Minister of Health for his region, could not come.

His absence would prove to be our misfortune.

"But these papers were prepared by the Ministry of Health," I pleaded. Bob, too, gave his two cents worth, which, by the look on the officer's face, was all it was worth. Our translator interpreted our fading pleas as my former confidence dissolved into the present reality.

Over the next half hour, much Russian gesticulation and hand waving by both the officers and our friends kept Bob and I in a not too uncomfortable darkness. It was, after all, something not unexpected. Far before the conclusion of the conversations, Bob and I both knew that the bags and boxes would not go with us, at least not today. But our confidence remained in the God who was well able to deliver both us and our boxes from the present circumstances.

Serge disappeared with the officers to secure the boxes in a safe area. This was our chance to discover from our interpreter that the papers were indeed valid. The problem was that they were prepared in Nikolaev and we were standing in Odessa. We would need to get a signature from the customs house here in Odessa for legal entry of our supplies. The Soviets no longer ruled the Ukraine (at least not in name), but their bureaucratic legacy lives on to dictate social order.

The customs house at the Port of Odessa proved to be of no surprise. Only a lone guard within the front foyer remained on duty. He of course was reluctant to affix his signature allowing the release of our supplies, which to him was potential contraband.

"He is just a little man of no authority," our interpreter explained as we drove towards Nikolaev. Our medical supplies remained in Odessa locked, supposedly, within a customs warehouse. Behind our car in the trailer, meant for the medical supplies, was my lone bag of personal effects. "After all," our interpreter explained, "with everyone home for the holiday, there is little that he could do."

A few moments passed as Bob and I silently looked at each other thinking the same thing. "What holiday?" I asked.

"Why Pentecost, of course."

4 JUNE

He wants to know what is your mission. He wants to know what you intend to do in the Ukraine." Genna, my interpreter had turned towards me from his place in the front passenger seat of the Lada. Serge was intent on the road and any one of the perils he may encounter as he drove us back to Odessa: rocks, potholes, bumps, and policemen. I would only later comprehend the hazard these policemen, relics of the soviet era, posed with their occasional checkpoints and striped batons.

In the backseat beside me was Dr. Peter Snisarenko, the Deputy Minister of Health for the Nikolaev region. Gennadi had been talking to him in Russian immediately before he had turned to me.

Jetlag was hitting me with waves of fatigue. I had arisen at 6:00AM to meet Dr. Snisarenko, or Dr. Peter as he was commonly referred, at the hospital. However, Dr. Peter was delayed due to his need to be at the bedside of a young 16 year old female who had suddenly collapsed on the street the evening before. Ultimately, she was diagnosed and Dr. Peter was summoned. She had suffered an intracranial bleed. To compound her troubles, she had been unfortunate enough to suffer her malady in a city of 800,000 (and a region of well over 1.5 million) without a neurosurgeon. Dr. Peter's trip to Odessa would now accomplish a dual purpose: retrieve our medical supplies and convince a neurosurgeon to come back with us.

We had waited outside the hospital where I intermittently napped inside the Lada. My ability to sleep in almost any position (a feat that I had perfected in medical school) was augmented by my fatigue. After an hour, Dr. Peter surfaced and we accompanied him to his office at the Ministry of Health. There we met his boss, the Regional Medical Director, and then waited for him in his office as he collected his papers needed for our appeal in Odessa.

I sat by the window overlooking the tree-lined street. The window sill was three to four feet thick, a loud hint of cold, harsh winters. The ceiling above was lined with a border of ornate plaster flowers. From these, pale yellow walls descended to wooden panels of similar color which rose approximately five feet from the wooden floors, also of corresponding color. Along the walls, wires which supplied electrical outlets descended from above. Fortunately, there was no associated blackened area as I had seen at the airport terminal. The room was furnished with a lone desk, a long conference table and accompanying chairs, a small wooden cabinet, and a refrigerator. On each were piles of papers through which Dr. Peter was shuffling.

A knock at the double doors was followed by entry of a tall thin woman with red hair and a red dress. She was followed by an older woman. Dr. Peter turned from his paper search and arose to greet them. Soon, we were both looking at X-rays of a broken humerus in which a rod had been surgically inserted for stabilization. Apparently, Dr. Peter, an orthopedist and dermatologist, was asked to provide an opinion about the arm of the older woman's husband. Her furrowed brow revealed the obvious concern which was only partially relieved when Dr. Peter reassured her. Reluctantly, and full of questions, she was led out to the dark hallway by the woman in red.

Dr. Peter spoke to Genna. Genna then turned to me. "She requests Dr. Peter's opinion about the work of another surgeon."

Ultimately, after a few more interruptions, we ventured out to the Lada parked on the sidewalk under the locust trees. Serge turned the key. The Lada responded. We bounced over the curb and then over cobblestone sidestreets dissected by a multitude of tram tracks. It was a relief to finally reach a smooth asphalt avenue leading to the bridge. After crossing the river and maneuvering beyond a police checkpoint, Dr. Peter began his questioning of my motives. By this time we were cruising through wheat fields and past cherry tree orchards. Poplar, locust, white maple, Russian olive, and willow trees intermittently lined our route casting tranquility, uncommon in the city, upon our small vehicle.

"I am here because I have heard about your difficulties," I answered.

Before I could proceed, Dr. Peter spoke once again, this time in broken English which at times required clarification by Genna. He spoke of his country which formerly was a world power. He recounted his experiences as a Soviet medical advisor to Vietnam and Angola. He also mentioned his time in France where he had received additional medical training.

"You are from a great country," he said somewhat tremulously. "We appreciate you coming to help us. Because our country was once great...and that we even helped others, like Vietnam and Angola, it is very difficult for us to accept our current condition. It is difficult for us, as physicians, to treat our patients without proper medical supplies." After a long pause, he added, "It is difficult for us to ask for help because of our pride."

After a brief hesitation in which Dr. Peter regained his composure, he continued. "But it is more difficult to watch people die, so on behalf of all Ukraine, I appreciate you coming to us."

He had tears in his eyes. I wondered how many had suffered because he and his colleagues did not have the necessary medicines and supplies. I wondered how many had died.

"Like I said, I heard about your difficulties. But as you know, I am not a representative of my government." I paused to make sure he understood. "I am a lone physician with a private practice back in America. When I heard about your problems I prayed. God gave me an abundance of medical supplies in response. I am here to give them to you, provided we are successful at clearing customs."

After the interpretation from Genna, he turned directly to me, grasped my hand and declared, albeit haltingly, in English, "Thank you! We get supplies today!" His demeanor had changed from helplessness to determination.

"I would also, as you know, like to set up a temporary clinic sponsored by the Church as well as provide any assistance to the medical community in my field of infectious disease."

Through Genna he indicated such would be very welcome since the AIDS epidemic had reached their district. He revealed that there were well over 1700 known cases of frank AIDS in the city of 800,000. He also indicated that from time to time they were forced to fight off epidemics of older diseases with very limited resources. I recalled the epidemic of Cholera reported by health officials a year ago in this very district.

"Also, I would like to demonstrate to everybody that God is alive and is interested in meeting your needs."

Dr. Peter grasped my hand and turned to Genna. Genna turned to me with the interpretation. "He says you have demonstrated that God is what you say just by coming to our impoverished land."

Suddenly the constant drone of the engine changed pitch. All eyes looked ahead. From my seat I could see several uniformed policemen pointing their black and white striped batons directly at us. There seemed to be a sudden flurry of anxiety among my fellow passengers as each spoke hurriedly to each other. Behind the policemen was their crude cement block station. Nearby was a car on top of cement pilings twenty feet above road level. It had obviously been in an accident as the front end was smashed causing the crumpled hood to point skyward. The tires had collapsed flat on the pilings. Windows were absent except for a few sharp fragments of windshield near the hood. The entire vehicle was black, charred from fire.

Serge opened his door to step out, offering his papers to the approaching officer. Dr. Peter, his expression quite serious, motioned for me to open my door. In his right hand he shoved his red passport across my lap towards the same policeman. The policeman's eye was directed towards this red book, on which gold letters, "CCCP" boldly embossed the cover.

A flurry of Russian went back and forth with me in the middle. Soon I heard, "...Amerikanski Dr. Price...." as Dr. Peter pointed in my direction. For a brief moment, I wondered whether I was being implicated or lauded.

Whatever the method, it worked for we were soon back on the road.

With the policemen in our dust, I finally asked Genna about the car on the pilings.

"That," he responded, "is what happens to you if you don't stop."

Many kilometers later, the traffic congealed into thick molasses. Tall, worn-out apartment buildings lined the highway as we maneuvered through greater Odessa. Today, unlike yesterday, people were out in full force. Scores awaited buses or trams. Others congregated near kiosks hoping for good prices. Sellers hawked what appeared to be black sunflower seeds, red cherries, cold bread, and coca-cola. Smokers discarded cigarette butts as they waited their turn to buy or ride. On every corner the Kwas tank emptied its fare to thirsty consumers. Considering that Kwas was the fermentation product of moldy bread, I could think of a thousand other ways to quench my thirst on a hot day.

Our first destination was the Port of Odessa. Serge finally pulled the Lada onto the sidewalk to park after searching for several minutes amongst the snail-paced traffic. As Dr. Peter and Serge strode towards the custom house, Genna and I settled down for the first of our many delays.

I awoke when Serge cranked the engine. With a jerk we pulled back out into the traffic. Soon we were higher up on the hill overlooking the port and Black Sea. Again, Serge traversed the curb to park on what I was learning to be his favorite parking spot, the sidewalk. No one seemed to care about his choice as they went about their respective business.

UKRAINE – JUNE 1996

"The Medical College," Genna explained as he motioned towards the tall stone buildings which even now Dr. Peter was rushing towards. Serge and Genna headed towards an ice cream vendor. I chose not to partake as I was considering the possible infectious complications of such action. Medical students, professors, and doctors in training milled about the wide, tree-shaded sidewalk. Many were in white smocks and caps of their profession. Others congregated, I suppose much like those of my medical class, asking questions about recent exams or a fresh dissection.

I decided to measure the time by the number of ice cream bars ingested by Serge. The count was four when Dr. Peter returned to invite us in. Once inside, my pupils took several moments to adjust to the shadows. These moments allowed Dr. Peter a head start up the stone steps directly before me. On the third floor, a statue of a balding Hippocrates stared blankly beside his oath chiseled in the stone wall. The light was better up here. Skylights overhead were far superior to the dim lightbulbs of the floors below. Suddenly, we were walking through a classroom of students bent over their wooden benches, some with notes, others with partially dissected rats, which I assumed to be of good supply. Once back in the hall, I looked up towards the upper wall to see mug shots of what I assumed to be professors. Not one wore a smile.

I wouldn't have been surprised if behind the next door I would have seen Pavlov and his dog. However, the next door led to a restroom of sorts with stagnant water in a basin, and smelly holes in the floor.

I quickly exited to find Dr. Peter talking with one of those pictured above. I assumed him to be the neurosurgeon we had come to fetch. Dr. Peter did his best to cordially introduce me. However, the professor seemed a bit too preoccupied to notice as he turned back towards his classroom.

Soon we were back in traffic headed for our next stop, the airport. Once there, I settled down into my comfortable position in the backseat, while Genna did the same in the front. Dr. Peter and Serge headed inside to resume the negotiations. Not too much time passed when they returned. Our next stop was at a gatehouse within a wooded area nearby.

Many cars were parked on the side of the street. However, once again, Serge found a spacious spot on the sidewalk. A red and white gate halted the flow of traffic on the roadway. I was imagining myself in a John leCarre spy novel when our cohorts returned, the gate was electronically lifted, and we were allowed to proceed.

Finally, we had been allowed into the warehouse grounds where our medical supplies were held. My hopes were high that we would soon be back on the road towards Nikolaev with our supplies in the trailer behind us. When we pulled up again, as usual, to a nice piece of sidewalk, I noticed many people loitering about. Some were sitting inside their vehicles. Others had parked themselves under a shade tree. Still others lay sleeping on the grass. This should have been my clue that our ordeal was far from over.

Nevertheless, God turned our importunity to my opportunity to catch some much needed sleep. I knew He would deliver us and our supplies. He hadn't brought us this far to leave us. We simply had to play out this bureaucratic game.

While I slumbered, Serge and Dr. Peter haggled over nuances. I dozed on as Dr. Peter's patience wore thin. I entered into REM sleep and Serge argued.

Ultimately, however, we won the game.

Once inside the warehouse, I identified the duffel bags and cardboard boxes. We loaded. We left. Two sets of gates closed behind us. Ahead of us were several hours of rough road. Behind us were 12 hours of tribulation. But in our trailer bounced the medical supplies that would turn a city towards God. I was sure of it because, after all, it was Pentecost.

5 JUNE

"What are these?" She was holding a bottle of ampicillin capsules while Genna interpreted her Russian.

"Antibiotics for the children," I answered.

"And these?" Again she waited for the interpretation.

"Multivitamins for the elderly," was my reply.

Box by box, bottle by bottle, she inspected our supplies. She wore glasses and a blue uniform with a billed cap. Her brown straight hair dangled below her shoulders as she leaned over the trailer digging deep into the boxes for the next suspicious bottle.

I had been in my usual position since 6:00AM, the back seat of the Lada which, of course, was parked on the sidewalk. Gennadi and I had been dozing, as was my habit of late, when Serge returned with the officer from the customs house in Nikolaev. We had cleared customs in Odessa yesterday on the condition that we present ourselves to their compadres here in Nikolaev this morning. There was simply no getting around this Soviet style bureaucracy. But it wasn't a total loss as I was catching up on sleep.

UKRAINE – JUNE 1996

It was our hope that we would be able to clear this final hurdle so that the free clinic could begin as scheduled today. It was already past the planned starting time, yet I was sure that our patients would wait. After all, in my experiences, time and schedules are only relative, unless of course you live in the United States.

A second officer approached with a sauntering gait. He began poking his nose around as I was being grilled by his cohort. Until now, I had little anxiety. But with an extra gruff officer, I wondered about our chances. I suppose he had the authority to confiscate every item and the connections to find a good price on the black market.

He spoke and I waited for the interpretation.

"He wants to know if you have blood pressure medications," Genna reported.

I answered in the affirmative.

"He wants to know if he can have some," was Genna's interpretation of the officer's mumblings.

I don't know if I was being asked to bribe the officer, or if he, like almost everyone else here in the Ukraine, was simply desperate for medical care. I only knew what my answer would be.

"Most certainly!" Come to our free clinic sponsored by Bethany Church and I will not only give you the medication you have requested, but a free exam and any other medications you may require. Bring your family as well. I'll do the same for them."

I don't know if my response had anything to do with the next event. But the female officer immediately cut off the inspection, stamped the necessary paper, and apologized for the delay.

In the midst of a flurry of "spaciba's (thank's)" on our part, we packed up and headed towards the clinic.

Across town, they were waiting. The cinema had been loaned to Bethany Church for the occasion. In the not so distant future, the city would loan this very building for an even greater purpose. But today I had no knowledge of the future. I simply had ten boxes of medical supplies and a crowd that needed them.

Fifty-nine frightened Ukrainians would feel my stethoscope. Dr. Peter's patient who collapsed on the street and for whom we had gone to the medical school in Odessa in search of a neurosurgeon, would not have this privilege.

The neurosurgeon could not come. The fifty-nine had waited months and even years for this opportunity. The girl who remained comatose, would wait longer.

But they were nervous. Many broke out into tears as I entered the exam areas. They were afraid of what I might find. Chernobyl was on everyone's mind.

"Oh, Doc...." Serge left his sentence unfinished as he searched for the English equivalent of his Russian thoughts. Abandoning the effort, he turned to Tatyana, who was serving as my interpreter for the day.

"Serge said that a doctor from the Infectious Disease Hospital called. He heard that you were in town and wants to meet you," Tatiana rapidly and assuredly exclaimed. As one of the top English teachers in Nikolaev, she had a way of commanding attention.

"Let's make it tonight," I answered from my place in the backseat of the Lada as we headed back towards the house. Liuba, Serge's wife, would be waiting for us there. Once we arrived, she would set the table under the veranda just outside the summer kitchen. There would be fruit from her garden (which at this time of year included strawberries and the ever plentiful cherries), salami, soup, bread, and a main course. She rarely served the ubiquitous borchst, so common in the Ukraine. Instead, she presented recipes from her native Siberia.

Liuba and Serge had opened their home to all four of us. Bob and his wife, Sylvia, slept in the master bedroom. I on the living room couch, and Rich Maring in the spare room. Serge and Liuba slept in the small room off the inside kitchen with their two small children. Liuba cooked our meals, boiled our water, and tidied our rooms. Serge thought of everything else, including rigging a gas heater to provide hot showers. This was quite a feat when the rest of the town went without electricity and running water more often than not. Serge also was responsible for most of our transportation. This was a herculean task in a country where most gas stations were buying only, and not selling. I marvelled at how Serge had modified the Lada to also run on propane when gasoline was scarce.

There were hotels in Nikolaev. I had been told by many that they were as cozy as the best gulag in the old Soviet Union with service to boot (no pun intended). Even the Lufthansa agents in Frankfurt had warned me, "...if you stay in a hotel, don't open the door to any knock unless you are expecting company. You could be robbed, mugged, or worse. There are elements in the Ukraine that thrive on your misfortune...."

I was pleased to be under Serge and Liuba's roof.

UKRAINE – JUNE 1996

The Infectious Disease Hospital was close to the zoo. After a few inquiries, we found Dr. Antoly Vucholovski. We followed him through dark hallways into a patient's room after the usual introductions. "He came in just a few days ago," Gennadi interpreted Dr. Vucholovski's description of the patient before us. The doctor was a burly bearded Ukrainian. A touch of gray accented his brown curly hair as he explained the circumstances about the young man confined to the hospital bed. As he talked, I looked on the bedside clipboard to see measurements of hemoglobin, leukocytes, and kidney function. My college Russian was coming back as I slowly sounded out each cyrillic character. Beyond the clipboard was the furrowed sweaty brow of one critically ill boy. His eyes betrayed fear; a flushed complexion his anemia; and blood red but jaundiced conjunctiva his diagnosis. He had Leptospirosis and he was in big trouble.

The corkscrew shaped bacteria, called a spirochete, was attacking vociferously. Despite intravenous fluids and large doses of penicillin, his liver and kidneys had already suffered significant insult. Bloody conjunctiva were a sign of similar pathology in all his mucosal surfaces; all were oozing blood and protein. His life, like his serum, was slipping away.

Dr. Vucholovski was explaining his plan of treatment. But we both knew that this young man, who had unfortunately been exposed to infected rat urine, may not survive. I silently prayed for a miracle.

Down the corridor, out of earshot of the patient, I began, "I brought with me some supplies that I believe you will find useful. God has provided and we want you to have them. If you have many more patients like the one I just saw, I imagine you could use them."

By this time we were in his office, sitting on chairs that just recently were the domain of papers and journals. I further explained that a container of supplies shipped months earlier had arrived in Odessa and was due in Nikolaev any day. I assured him that he would receive a good share.

"Spaciba!" He shouted in his deep baritone and clasped my hand with both of his.

The emotion of the moment passed. I arose to leave.

But the doctor turned quickly to Genna speaking in urgent tones. Genna interpreted, "Don't you want to see the AIDS ward?"

"Of course!"

We all donned white smocks and headed to another building hidden in the trees, dodging the large water puddles enroute. There was a guard at the door who allowed our entry after a moment's hesitation.

"Pazshalusta." Dr. Antoly invited us in with an outstretched arm.

We entered into a dark chamber past iron bars. In the dim hallway to the left, behind another set of bars, I recognized as the nurses' station. To the right, file cabinets encroached upon the murky hall leading to patient rooms. We could see a few thin patients leaning against the bars of the far window. Cigarettes in hand, they conspicuously peered our way. We entered their 10 foot by 20 foot room. There were four beds, three of which were occupied by thin girls. Their makeup was layered and mascara thick. After cursory introductions I asked if I could pray. They allowed it, I did it, and then I turned to leave.

"Come back!"

It was Genna. "The one in black wants to ask you a question."

"Doctor?" She asked in Russian. She was visibly trembling. "They have told us many things here in this country." Her tone was full of sarcasm. It was quite obvious to me, even though I could not understand completely her Russian, that she was sick and tired of games and wanted the truth. Facing terminal illness as she was had given her a new perspective on life's games. Her trembling transiently ceased as she continued. "But I want to know from you, is there any drug, either here or in America, that can help me? You see, they have told me that I have AIDS and that I will die very soon...."

Tears filled her eyes and her trembling returned but much more evident. Genna's slow and deliberate interpretation of her Russian also translated her despair.

"Unfortunately, there is no proven cure at this time despite all the efforts of your doctors here in the Ukraine as well as those in America. We do have some drugs that can treat some of your symptoms and infections. We even have some drugs that can slow the virus down. But we do not, as of yet, have a sure cure."

She immediately collapsed onto her bed. It was as if my words had knocked her breath away. After a few moments she looked up. Through her tears and running mascara, she pleaded, "Is there then no hope for me?"

I paused. She now looked much different. Before, she was one who had seen life at its worst. She was angry. She was bitter. She was sarcastic. She was in control.

UKRAINE – JUNE 1996

Now as she looked up at me, I recognized her as one whose dreams lay shattered. Maybe not too long ago her childhood dreams of happiness and acceptance had been drowned out by promises now obviously unfulfilled. She was someone's little girl, desperately crying for help.

I bent down and said as gently as I could, "Oh, but there is hope. There is always hope. Jesus Christ is our hope."

Genna explained about Jesus in a rapid sequence of Russian. She soon was back on her feet and her tears had been wiped away. The joy of the Lord was in her heart.

Again I turned to go. Again Genna stopped me. "Dr. Price! Another one wants to hear about Jesus!" Genna was motioning to a blond girl just rising to her feet from her position closer to the window. I turned to see her as she looked with pleading eyes, not towards me, but towards the One who sent me.

6 JUNE

"More kamput?"

I looked up to see Liuba with her flask of plum juice that had been diluted with boiled water. I accepted another glass and turned again to my rice boiled in goat's milk.

Breakfast had been in full swing when I arrived. Rich Maring, Bob and Sylvia Greiner, and Serge were already sitting at the table under the grape arbor just outside the summer kitchen. They had been up for some time. I still had not acclimated to the time change.

"Doctor Price, I presume!" Rich had roared. Rich had been here in Nikolaev the longest, arriving weeks before. Then came Bob and Sylvia days later. They had been teaching, preaching and encouraging the local Christians. God had been openly at work through their ministry: the brokenhearted had been healed, the oppressed had been freed, those who had been bruised by years of atheism had seen God work visibly for the first time.

Rich had been preaching almost nonstop since his arrival. His raspy greeting today attested this fact. The Ukrainians loved him and hungered after his every word which God used to bring deliverance and healing. Bob and Sylvia were seasoned warriors. In the early days, they had traveled the country by rail and had experienced other inconveniences. More recent trips had been a bit easier but still spiritually difficult. I had heard their stories and found myself wondering whether I could have endured as they had. Endure they did and now they were seeing all God had promised.

"A little bit of Pentecost at the hospital last night, eh?" Rich slapped me on the back and then continued. "Serge here tells us that some of the patients received the Lord!"

"Yeah, it was a little bit exciting."

"A little bit exciting?! Doctor, do you realize what's happening here?" Bob was again bringing us back to reality. After all, he had a better sense for the Ukrainians than any of us. "People are openly showing some emotion which just does not happen here. It has to be God! Now, Serge indicates that the same is occurring in the hospitals. And by the way, who is this Dr. Vucholovski anyway?"

"I don't know. Ask Serge."

"Well, Serge, who is he...the Doctor at the hospital?" Bob redirected the question. Genna provided the interpretation through a mouthful of bread and sausage.

"He doesn't really know, except that a friend of his...the Doctor's...told him about Dr. Price."

"I think we should all go back," I interrupted. "I think we should all go back to the hospital and witness to the rest of the patients. Not all of them heard."

"I was thinking the same," Bob said as he turned to Genna once again. "Ask Serge if he can arrange another visit for all of us."

Hours later we were back at the cinema. We would eventually examine and treat sixty-six. One of these was a woman in which Rich, for some reason unknown to me at the time, had a particular interest. She was middle aged and a little heavy. Her eyes were full of foreboding as she was ushered behind the curtain. Tatyana spoke to her and handed me her paper that revealed her complaints, most of which I could not decipher. "What's her problem?"

"She has a mass...a tumor."

"Where?"

"Here."

My exam revealed nothing.

"Where did you say?" I asked again.

"There."

UKRAINE – JUNE 1996

Again I could not find it. Once again I asked. Once again I could not find it.

"Is she sure she has a mass?" As I asked the question, I wondered whether she was one of those who insisted upon having an abnormality when there was nothing to be found.

Tatyana replied, "She is sure she had it."

"What do you mean, had?" I asked as I walked around the curtain and towards the next patient. As I did, I nearly ran into Rich as he was eavesdropping on our conversation. I soon found myself surrounded by the others, all with a strange look about them.

"You can't find it can you, Doc?" Rich blurted out.

"Can't find what?"

"The mass," Rich almost exploded.

"What's going on?" My question was answered only by goofy grins and twinkling eyes. Since no one answered my question in words that I could understand, I decided to answer theirs. After all, there was a long line of Ukrainians just outside the door expecting the Amerikanski doctor to attend to their respective ills. I had little time for psychoanalysis.

"There is no mass and there is no tumor."

"There is no mass?" Rich asked.

I paused. I surmised that maybe Rich had been drinking some bad kamput and thereby his hearing had been affected.

"NO mass and NO tumor," I expressed with the emphasis on both "NO's".

Abruptly, Rich screamed and Bob smiled. The grin an Sylvia's face was from ear to ear. Tatyana turned to the patient and jabbered to her in Russian. Immediately the patient placed her hands together beneath her chin and with tears looked heavenward.

"We didn't want to tell you before," Rich hoarsely explained. "We didn't want to sway you one way or the other. We wanted an unbiased medical opinion. She's the one we told you about. She's the one who had a tumor the size of a grapefruit that the doctors wanted to cut out. But then a few nights ago we laid hands on her and prayed. Now, it really is gone! Hallelujah!"

That night I gave my testimony to about three hundred. The woman without the mass was in the front row. Her hands were still folded under her chin. Her teary eyes gazed towards heaven.

7 JUNE

Boris stood before me. He had shocking white hair that stood out straighter than an arrow, each strand pointed in a different direction. His mustache was also white, the strands of which also haphazardly shot out from follicles refusing to be trained. His eyes were jovial; his grin, infectious. But I was drawn to his shirt, or rather, that which was pinned to his shirt. Several rows of medals pinned just above his pocket had drawn my attention.

He had reflexively unbuttoned the top two buttons and drew back his shirt with both hands. I placed my stethoscope on his revealed bare skin to listen to a regular thumping heart tone. I subsequently discovered his blood pressure to be slightly elevated and pus on his posterior pharyngeal wall. From Tatyana I discovered he was already taking something for his blood pressure. I, therefore, prescribed amoxicillin for sinusitis.

Again my attention was on his medals. He was obviously retired after some years of service to his country. He was a pensioner: one of those groups reported by recent American news media to be disaffected by change. This was so because his pension now barely covered the apartment rental, much less the necessities of food and fuel. Some months, however, the government didn't have the money to pay even this paultry sum.

"Ask him if his medals are for bravery." A bigger smile burst across his face when Tatyana delivered my question. He grabbed my hand with both of his and pumped them up and down quite forcibly. His eyes literally sparkled with joy as he now began rattling off Russian with great animation. Bob and Rich caught me trying to politely extricate myself from his vise-like grip as we both exited from behind the curtain. Whatever he was saying caused Tatyana to giggle a hurried response. Finally, she grabbed his hand and pried me loose.

"What was that all about?" Rich asked with a smirk.

"Nothing," I paused. "Just an old KGB buddy."

Over one hundred patients later, I sought the solace of a soft chair. Over forty of these patients experienced Christ for the first time. Pastor Greeshan and other local Christians who had volunteered their services to make the clinic a success were seeing firsthand the fruit of their labors. Their neighbors were being helped not only physically but also spiritually.

Slavik also was excited. Because his stand for Christ had preceded the breakup of the former Soviet Union, Slavik had suffered through much turmoil and persecution. Ultimately, he was allowed to emigrate to the USA in the early

UKRAINE – JUNE 1996

1990's, where he now lived with his immediate family. Yet he spent much of his time back here in Nikolaev, the city of his upbringing. Before his emigration (I wondered whether it was voluntary) he had been responsible for the establishment of several Churches, which still looked to him for spiritual guidance. He, therefore, returned frequently to guide them. He also did all he could to facilitate delivery of food, clothing, and medical supplies to help his Ukrainian brothers and sisters in need.

"Would you like to see a little of our place?" Slavik asked.

"Certainly!" I volunteered despite my weariness. Bob, Sylvia and Rich, however, having seen the sights previously, decided to head back to the house.

I was directed to Serge's car parked on the plaza just outside the cinema under the trees. Slavik slid into the seat beside me in the back while Tatyana occupied the passenger seat next to Serge.

Immediately Slavik leaned forward to get Serge's attention and pointed to the left. Serge nodded and Tatyana giggled her approval.

Slavik turned to me. "We will show you land that government gave us for our Church. We have five acres here within walking distance of 60,000 apartment dwellers."

Serge had eased the car into gear and we were approaching what appeared to be a park. Trees lined the sidewalk, on which Serge had maneuvered the car. As we rode, pedestrians were quickly rushing to avoid Serge's progress. Yet they appeared neither irritated nor surprised. I marveled not only at the beautiful park setting but also Serge's choice of roadway. Had we been in America, Serge would have received a far different reception from these pedestrians.

"The Orthodox priest became very upset with government when he heard about their decision to give us this land," Slavik continued. "But the mayor said the deal was done."

"Why did the mayor give you the land?" I asked.

"Because we bring food, clothing, and medicines. Also, we agreed to buy an apartment for the three squatter families that have lived here in the park. The last family will move out this week so we can begin construction of security wall around the property."

Serge made a U-turn where the sidewalk flared out and headed back towards the cinema.

"We are quite happy," Slavik mentioned with pride. "We will be able to build a big Church here someday."

"When do you break ground?"

"When we get enough building materials. Some materials come from government in appreciation for medical supplies and food that we bring from America. Other supplies we must buy. Unfortunately, we do not have enough supplies nor money to buy yet. So we wait."

Up ahead a gaudy statue, typical of the communist era with several workers struggling against the elements, rose above the trees. I leaned to my right towards the window to get a better look.

Recognizing my interest, Slavik said, "Do you like our monuments?"

I didn't immediately answer, except with a smile. I was thinking of the many memorials I had seen here in the city. Even the statues depicting selfless workers sacrificing for the good of the State couldn't fool the people forever. They now were unkempt, surrounded by weeds. The one up ahead was not dissimilar.

"Let's show him the memorial downtown," Slavik spoke in English to Tatyana for my benefit.

"Oh, I do believe Dr. Price will enjoy it!" Tatyana responded with a smile.

Slavik leaned forward, instructing Serge in Russian. Quickly, the engine roared and we were off the sidewalk and back on the street. We dodged streetcars, trucks, and other cars along the busy thoroughfare running north of the cinema. A turn to the left brought us to a cobblestone sidestreet that was dissected by trolley tracks. We crossed these tracks several times before we were deposited on smoother pavement. Tall apartment buildings of similar disrepair were on both sides. I was busy inspecting the tops of these edifices and therefore was not prepared when the car lurched.

Serge had found the potholes, which redirected my attention towards the road. Up ahead, a large structure rose to the sky in the middle of the road. I saw a gargantuan Cossack, dressed in a medieval helmet and robe dwarfing the surrounding trees. One fist grasped a raised sword while the opposite arm bore a shield. I imagined him as Vlad the Impaler commanding an imaginary army.

"No, this is not the memorial I had in mind," Slavik chuckled as he perceived my interest. "We have a little ways more to go."

Soon, we were on the finest street in town, Lenin Prospect. It was bordered on the sides with brick and stone buildings of the business section, whereas the central boulevard was landscaped with flowers and scotch pines. Slavik suddenly directed Serge to a small kiosk.

"I'll be right back," Slavik instructed.

He returned shortly with a liter bottle of Coca-cola.

"A little present for Rich," Slavik indicated. "I think he is growing tired of our kamput."

The soft drink cost 250,000 coupons; quite an expensive item for the average Ukrainian. But for me, it represented only $1.50.

Back in the car, Slavik gave a few more instructions and we were presently at our destination.

"Let's get out." Tatyana and I obediently disembarked at Slavik's instructions. On the left was a park with the usual complement of shade trees. At the far end was an iron railing beyond which was the dark blue waters of the Juznyj Bug River. On our right was the street bordered by a tall stone building.

"We will walk to the front of the government building to see our memorial," Slavik indicated. He then added, "You know, I spent many days and nights in this building prior to the breakup. All at the invitation of the KGB. My memories, as you can imagine, are not so pleasant."

I considered for a moment whether to ask details, but then decided against it.

Our progress soon brought us onto a square directly in front of the government building. The square's nucleus was dominated by a tall statue.

"This is our memorial," Slavik interrupted my investigation.

I walked around to the front. The granite base was a good forty feet high and the man above was at least three times that. I recognized Lenin before I read the cyrillic script on the granite pedestal. His eyes were piercing yet empty. His scowl only accentuated his cold, heartless but hollow glare. He was wearing an overcoat and a shlapka, a fur hat.

"Some believe that before he died he recognized he had made a mistake. They say he was even searching the scriptures."

Tatyana quickly added to my commentary, "Yes, but the seminarian ended any thought of mistakes."

I knew she was referring to Stalin and his series of pogroms.

There was an uneasy silence until Slavik, who had remained silent, turned my attention back to the river. We strolled back to the railing. At the bottom of the bluff, a large factory lay gleaming in the afternoon sun. Cranes stood silent, chimneys were smokeless.

"This is Nikolaev's famous shipyards. Because of them, Nikolaev was a closed city."

"What do you mean, closed?" I asked.

Slavik continued. "It means that nobody except those with special clearance could visit here."

"Yes, and even those who lived here had to have special permission to leave," Tatyana added. "We were very much isolated."

"Why was that?" I asked.

"Because these factories built military vessels, among others," Slavik answered. "One hundred seventy five thousand people worked here at one time. Now, they are empty."

"Empty?"

"Yes. No one works here anymore."

I looked again. The tall rusting cranes and vacant docks spoke no more. The paranoia of the Soviet block begot one more empty industrial behemoth; a monument itself.

"Is there work elsewhere?" I asked.

"No. Only pensions that are too small. That is, when they are paid. There are some pensioners who have not been paid for months. The government simply does not have the money," Tatyana commented.

"That gives you an idea why the government appreciates our food and medical supplies. The people live by selling possessions. They have no extra to provide for their health."

After Slavik spoke, we turned silently back towards Lenin. Around his base, several women in peasant dress scurried about planting flowers. His blank eyes remained fixed, away from the shipyards, and towards the rotting apartment buildings.

Later that evening, I saw more eyes with empty stares. They were those of the AIDS patients. They were sightlessly staring at the floorboards of their prison, the Infectious Disease Hospital. We had been invited back and I had just spoken of God, and the hope He provides via His Son, Jesus. Yet the patients were unmoved. They had heard my words but their eyes betrayed that their hearts had not opened. I rephrased my words, with Tatyana's help. But it was to no avail.

Bob was at my side. "Let me give it a shot," he had said.

He expertly expounded the scriptures, revealing our God of compassion. Yet their eyes remained blank and their hearts hardened.

An uneasy silence prevailed. Someone shuffled their feet against the hard wooden floors.

Rich stepped forward. He would not go down easily. He reasoned further. Among other things, he pointed out to them that they had little to lose.

Nevertheless, they were willing to lose. Their eyes remained downcast.

I turned my back. The rooms were dark; the floors filthy. I wondered if I had done my best.

That was when I heard his words. They were a deep and rich baritone, forceful in delivery. He spoke their Russian. He addressed them from within their culture. His words entered their consciousness and I knew it from the moment he began, even though I understood little of his Russian.

Tatyana began whispering the interpretation and I heard him say, "...these men speak truth. But don't believe with your mind, believe with your heart. Take the first step...."

Suddenly, all eyes and hearts were open. Not only those of the patients, but also those of the nurses. They too had the tears and smiles that reveal opened hearts.

Not too much time went by when even the gruff guard tapped my shoulder. His Russian was much too fast. I responded the best I could, "...gavarite medlina (speak slowly)." But only Tatyana was able to clearly identify his purpose. "He, also, wants to receive Jesus as Lord," she said with considerable amazement.

Lenin's eyes were gone. No one had their emptiness when we left. Their's were the eyes of peace and joy. They had understood the Gospel message and had received it as their own. We left as brothers and sisters, not as foreigners.

The baritone words of truth were spoken by one I had not even known to be a Believer.

Dr. Vucholovski had revealed his true colors.

8 JUNE

"Maybe it should be a forty foot."

"Forty foot?" I asked incredulously.

Then for an instant, I contemplated the possibility. Previously, I had agreed to ship a twenty foot container full of medical supplies directly from Houston. Now, as I was discussing the specifics with Slavik, he had suggested doubling the size.

We were sitting underneath the grapevines near Serge's summer kitchen. Liuba and her helpers, including the 'pizza lady', were busy preparing the noon meal. Bob, Sylvia, and Rich were sitting with us. They had introduced me to the neighbor known as the 'pizza lady' because of her recipe. Even Liuba referred to her as such when she talked to us in her broken English. Evidently, on previous trips, the Amerikanskis preferred her pizza over the normal dinner-time fare (except for the one time on their last visit when she served up sardine and cream cheese pizza). But more importantly, she had recently recognized the power of God through Liuba's Christian witness.

Early morning sunlight filtered through the vines overhead as Slavik added, "Twenty foot would be good. You don't need to send forty foot. It's just that with every shipment of medical supplies or other relief, government gives building supplies for new church."

"By the way," he added, "the medical supplies you included in the container shipped in April cleared Odessa customs last week. We expect it here in a few days. What shall we do with the supplies?"

"Give them to Dr. Vucholovski. He needs them desperately."

Then it was my turn to add, "And we will ship a forty foot."

My faith had overtaken me. I believed God would supply in abundance. Before the year was out, God would indeed provide. We would send not one, but two forty foot containers with over a half million US dollars of essential medical supplies.

Dusk found us on the square in front of the cinema. I would be one of three to speak about Jesus. As they were setting up on the elevated steps surrounding the building, I milled about the crowd. I even walked down the street with Rich. As we did, we could estimate the reach of the public address system.

UKRAINE – JUNE 1996

On our way back towards the plaza, I heard a commotion behind me. I turned to see Boris. His medals were prominently displayed across his chest, again, on a striped shirt. He greeted me with his toothy smile while his two hands clutched mine. As he pumped, he talked. Not understanding many words, I, however, quickly began to discern the situation. With him was an elderly woman, a younger man, and a younger woman. Behind them were several children.

Tatyana came from behind to confirm my assumption, "He wants to introduce you to his family."

At that, they all in unison grinned, smiled, and nodded. Reflexively, without thinking, I did the same.

Boris and I had developed quite a friendship, even though I could understand little Russian and he comprehended no English. Yet we both understood the language of agape love. After I had examined him in the clinic, he had gone home and returned. In his hands were two books. The only English within these books was the inscription he had asked an interpreter to write, "Thank you very, very much for your help from KGB boy, Mazur Boris. Long live for our friendship." A very touching tribute from one who had so little to give, albeit in imperfect English.

Boris and his family began saying almost simultaneously, "Slava boho (Praise the Lord)!"

"Slava boho!" was my reply.

9 JUNE

I searched the crowd and I found them both. From my place behind Pastor Grecia, I spotted both Dr. Peter and Dr. Vucholovski among the three hundred plus in the packed lecture hall. I would soon use them as examples of those doing God's work at their respective places of employment. They were in the full-time ministry, I would say, even though they do not receive a pastor's salary. Thereby, I encouraged all to know their God, be strong, and do mighty exploits, right where they lived and right where they worked.

Afterwards, I made my way towards the back foyer. It was slow going because everyone wanted to stop and talk, even though most could not speak a word of English. I, of course, knew even less Russian. Nevertheless, I did a lot of smiling, grinning, and nodding.

"He's back here, just like I said."

"Where?"

"Over behind the counter by the coat rack," Tatyana answered. "You'll recognize his eyes."

I looked but I could not find him. Finally, I leaned way over the counter and saw his white bald head. His nose had been chipped, but his eyes were the same as those I had seen before, empty and sightless.

"An ignominious end, wouldn't you say?"

"But one well deserved!" piped in Rich who was approaching from the rear.

"Why is he here?" I asked.

"When we took over this former communist youth hall for our Church services, we thought it very unfitting for Lenin's bust to be on the stage with our Pastor. So we put him here."

Then as an afterthought, she added, "He now holds our coats while we preach the Gospel. Ironic, don't you think?"

Serge was waiting for us outside. Upon seeing us, he opened the doors of his car, parked in the shade and, as I had come to expect, on the sidewalk. Soon, we zipped through traffic towards our afternoon meal.

The apartment building appeared old. Fortunately, the electricity was working today and the lift was operational. After we entered, the shuddering, sluggish ascent made me wish that the electricity had been down. Finally, we arrived. The iron gate was folded to one side. I silently let my breath out between pursed lips as we touched solid cement once again.

The apartment consisted of four rooms, a luxurious suite according to Ukrainian standards. It also had a balcony, which in the winter was used as a deep freeze. Today, we simply savored the cool breeze and looked down to the bare earth below, a view similar to the one I had seen earlier in the week from the airplane.

In the diminutive kitchen, the tap produced water! What a day, both electricity and water!

My seat was on the couch. This put me at about eye level to the long dinner table spread with various Ukrainian culinary delights. There was stuffed cabbage, fresh cucumbers, sliced tomatoes, and cut salami. Of course, the most prominent dish was bread layered with heaping amounts of cream, topped off with sardines. The Ukrainians at the table eyed these with great anticipation. If I played my cards right, I surmised, these sardine tidbits would be long gone before being offered to me.

We ate what was set before us, albeit sparingly (knowing that if we were to make the fatal mistake of cleaning our plates like our mothers had taught, we would receive more). All this, we washed down cautiously with plum kamput.

The woman of the house had recently accepted Jesus into her heart after being healed of an emotional illness and accompanying chest pain. She ran home from Church on that day to get her husband. He was so shocked to see her running, that he went to the Church to investigate. His ailment, his doctors had said, was coronary artery disease. He too, was healed. When his arteries opened, so also did his heart to Jesus Christ.

Their way of saying thanks to those who had brought them the Gospel was this dinner. It was their very best and probably cost more than they could afford. But they revealed no hint of any sacrifice on their part as they served us graciously with great joy.

But God was not quite through with this family. After the meal, their teenage son and young adult daughter knelt to accept Jesus as Lord. The woman of the house wept profusely her tears of delight. The man, gruff and muscular, teared up as well, although a little more discreetly. But his elation was un-doubtedly the same, demonstrated by a broad smile from ear to ear.

Then I remembered again that it was Pentecost.

10 JUNE

We had an army of people and they were carrying in the boxes one at a time. Dr. Peter's office soon overflowed with bottles of antibiotics, boxes of syringes, and bags of gloves. Suddenly, a box tumbled from the table spilling out its contents of surgical drapes.

"No. Just leave it," I instructed several of the men who had rushed to retrieve the overturned container.

Slavik interpreted my request and the men went back through the door for additional loads.

Finally, the man with the last box struggled through the doorway. Dr. Peter questioned Slavik and upon receiving an answer, quickly darted down the dark hallway.

"He went to get his boss," Slavik reported.

"The Minister of Health?" I asked.

"Da," Serge answered.

My eyebrows rose. "You know more English than you let on, Serge," Bob chimed in to render my exact sentiments.

"Yeah, he's a sly dog," added Rich.

We had a good laugh. Serge, also, smiled sheepishly.

At that time the entourage entered. With Dr. Peter was the Minister of Health and several other doctors. One was the physician chosen to run the newly established AIDS clinic. The others went unidentified. The Minister of Health could be easily spotted because he was the only one with a tie, although no jacket.

After everyone entered, all movement stopped and every eye was upon me. I took this as my clue to begin speaking with Slavik as my interpreter.

"As you know, I am an American doctor. But what I want to make clear is that I do not represent the American government."

I stopped momentarily to allow Slavik to get it right in Russian.

"I heard about your difficulties so I wanted to do something to help. So I prayed."

I paused to let my words sink in.

"What you see here is God's answer." With that, I intentionally swept the room with my outstretched right arm. All around me was over $46,000.00 worth of medical supplies.

"What you see here, is not from the American government. It is from God. And that's not all. In a few days, a container will arrive with more supplies, also from God."

I said a few other things, the specifics of such I have forgotten, but the basic message was that Jesus Christ is alive. I then walked across the room, dodging the piles of supplies, directly to the Minister of Health. I wondered then, as I do now, how he attained his position. I assumed he had toed the party line and had been either an Agnostic or an Atheist. But today, his eyes were not the ones that I had seen on the many statues of Lenin. They were not sightless, piercing, and cruel. They lacked any evidence of hatred.

Today, as I shook his hand, his eyes were full of tears and thanksgiving.

UKRAINE – JUNE 1996

Later that day, I was seated at the window of my flight back to Frankfurt. We had already taxied to the very end of the runway when suddenly, all engines roared to life, catapulting us towards the Black Sea. Before the wheels left the ground I could see just off the tarmac in the grass the decrepit aircraft in disrepair just as I had seen upon arrival. Once in the air, I spotted the apartment buildings. Their appearance also had changed little. They all looked old even though some were still under construction. Finally, just before reaching the Black Sea coast, we passed over the cemeteries. From all physical appearances, nothing was different.

But I knew better.

Pentecost had made the difference.

It had made the difference not only here for Ukrainians, but also for Nepali orphans, Sri Lankan widows, and Brazilian slum dwellers. In the Philippines, fishermen, farmers, common laborers, and doctors were recognizing the Power behind Pentecost. Across India, those from all walks of life and castes experienced life changes of eternal proportions. Nepal's prison doors had fallen and Bulgaria's new day was on the horizon because of Pentecost. Even government officials, lawyers, housewives, and businessmen feel Pentecost's effects. It transcends all religions and all creeds in every race for every human being of every education level.

The seat belt light remained on as we gained altitude. I began to think about one of Jesus' parables. He had said, "...the kingdom of heaven is like a treasure hidden in a field, which a man found and hid; and for joy over it he goes and sells all that he has and buys that field."

I recalled the events of the past few days in the Ukraine: lives had been changed, hearts opened, and bodies had been healed. Then it suddenly hit me. God is that man! He was the man in the parable that found the field. The field is the world: the treasure its people. God sacrificed greatly for that field. He gave His only Son, Jesus to buy the field with its hidden treasure.

People are hidden because of rugged terrain, spiritual bondage, oppressive diseases, and political ideology. They are in darkness, remain afraid, and the night, as far as they are concerned, is rapidly falling. They are ignorant of the fact that each of them is so very special to God. They do not know that Jesus already has paid the price to allow them to be sons and daughters of the Most High God. Remote fields beyond far mountain ranges, wide oceans, and even cultural misunderstandings are not easily harvested. These are the devil's tools to keep the treasure hidden.

But God has answered the devil's tricks with Pentecost. He has empowered us with the Holy Ghost so that we can be used to seek out hidden treasure. God's desire is that everyone who is lost be found.

We were now well over the Black Sea, miles away from the Ukrainian shore. But I was confident God would have me return. I was assured that I would also be sent to other regions of the earth as well.

Because God has me searching for hidden treasure.